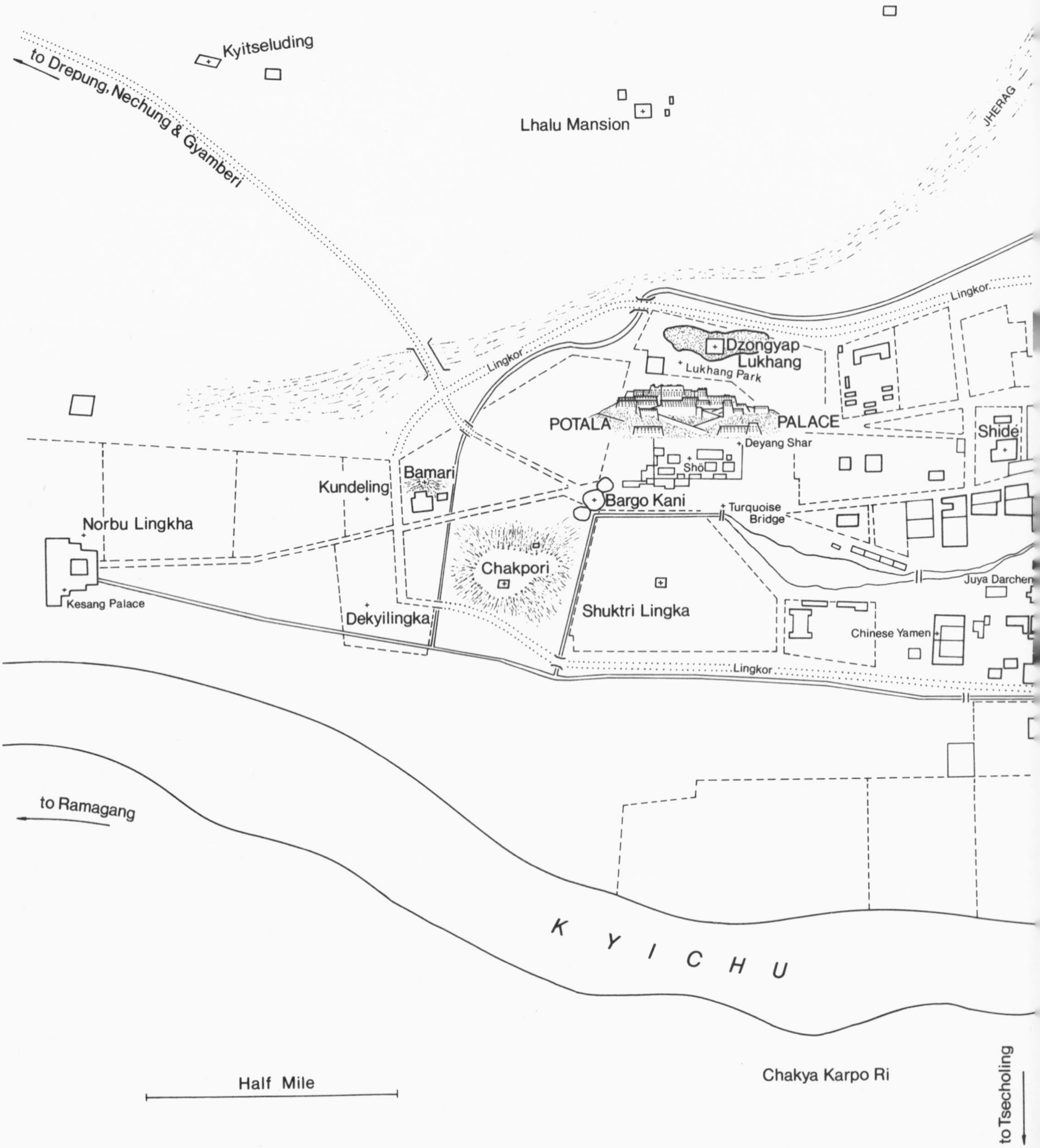

Kyitseluding
to Drepung, Nechung & Gyamberi
Lhalu Mansion
JHERAG
Lingkor
Dzongyap
Lukhang
Lukhang Park
Lingkor
POTALA
PALACE
Shide
Deyang Shar
Shö
Bamari
Kundeling
Bargo Kani
Turquoise
Bridge
Norbu Lingkha
Chakpori
Juya Darchen
Kesang Palace
Dekyilingka
Shuktri Lingka
Chinese Yamen
Lingkor
to Ramagang
K Y I C H U
Half Mile
Chakya Karpo Ri
to Tsecholing

LHASA and environs
with acknowledgement to Zasak Jigme Taring

CEREMONIES OF THE LHASA YEAR

Happy Birthday
Dear Martin –
with lots of love
From Marie Laure
and –

14th May 1984

Ceremonies of the Lhasa Year

Hugh Richardson

Edited by Michael Aris

Serindia Publications
London

ISBN 0 906026 29 6

First Published in 1993 by
Serindia Publications
10 Parkfields, London SW15 6NH

British Library Cataloguing in Publication Data
A catalogue record for this book is available
from the British Library

Printed by Biddles Ltd., Guildford

Contents

All photographs are by the author with the exception of the following which are either by or from the archives of; **Sir Charles Bell** [1920-21], by permission of the British Library, pages 88 above, 117 below: courtesy of the Pitt Rivers Museum, University of Oxford, pages 24, 28, 29, 70, 81, 88 below, 89 above, 97, 101, 107, 115; **Fondation Alexandra David-Neel** [1924?], pages 72-73; **Heinrich Harrer** [1946-50] pages, 21, 23, 31, 75, 78, 100, 120, 121; **Hopkinson Archive** [1926-28], courtesy of the Trustees of the British Museum, page 71; **Frederick Spencer Chapman** [1936-37] pages 15, 18, 53, 59, 90, 112, 117 above, 118, 119, 122; **Lt. Col. J.L.R. Weir** [1930-32] courtesy of the Royal Geographical Society, page 103. [Dates in square brackets refer to their visits to Tibet or the likeliest year of the photograph].

Introduction

The year at Lhasa was marked by a succession of ceremonies and festivals, some great state occasions, others of a lesser nature but all were either purposefully religious or reflected an awareness of religion; very few were purely secular. Although full of colour and spectacle, the great ceremonies were not mere pageantry but were essential rites for the well-being of Church and State and to be efficacious had to be performed strictly according to precedent. The whole official body had to attend; absence without good cause would be visited with severe penalties. The people of Lhasa and pilgrims from distant places came in large numbers to watch in spite of rough handling from the monk police to make them keep their distance; and from their quiet, respectful behaviour I believe that they felt that by their presence they were taking part in the ritual.

The origin of most of the ceremonies lies in the remote past but they have been rearranged and elaborated at different times, especially in the seventeenth century during the rule of the Great Fifth Dalai Lama and his equally great regent Sangye Gyatso when they were put into what was very much their latest form with the clear intention of enhancing the grandeur of the new regime imposed by the conquering army of the Oirad Mongol chieftain Gushri Khan, and the prestige and stability of the position of the Dalai Lama and the Gelukpa, Yellow Hat, church.

Lhasa is a striking setting for great occasions. Some took place within or at the foot of the Potala whose massive white and red façade, surmounted by gold pagoda roofs, towers majestically over the valley; others in front of and around the Jokhang, by comparison modest, almost humble to look at, hidden in the complex buildings of the Tsuklakhang, distinguished mainly by its golden roofs; but it is the ancient fountain-head of Buddhism in Tibet, numinous, profoundly impressive, its many altars glowing with butter-lamps and gold, a place of pilgrimage for people from all over the country. The wide street around the whole building and the courtyard in front provide space for prayer services and processions.

Many of the great ceremonies have been seen by foreign visitors who have left accounts of varying length and value. The most detailed include those by the Capuchin missionary, Father Cassiano Beligatti da Macerata, an intelligent observer who recorded what he saw in 1741-2; the Buriat Russian, G.T. Tsybikov in 1900 — he had the advantage of being a Buddhist with a knowledge of Tibetan; Sir Charles Bell in 1921; the adventurous Madame Alexandra David-Neel in 1924; F. Spencer Chapman in 1936; and Ernst Schäfer in 1939. Others who mention only salient features are the pandits Nain Singh and Kishen Singh ("A.K.") of the Survey of India in 1866 and 1878 respectively; Sir Henry Hayden and César Cosson in 1922; Heinrich Harrer from 1944 to 1950 — his photographs are particularly good; and T.L. Shen and S.C. Liu, also in the 1940s. No one, I think, has hitherto attempted a detailed description of all the ceremonies in their progression from month to month.

I had the good fortune to spend some nine years in Tibet between 1936 and 1950, mostly at Lhasa, as representative of the British Government of India and, later, of the independent Government of India. I was able to see the whole sequence of ceremonies in 1937, 1939 and 1947, and several of them in 1939, 1944, 1946 and 1950. When one was accepted by the officials of the Tibetan Government they always seemed eager that their guests should attend the ceremonies. They arranged seating with a good view but at a discreet distance, and they served tea, rice and noodles during the day-long performances. Although one had to be prepared to put up with cold conditions and sometimes dust storms during many of the ceremonies, they never lost their fascination. It was prudent to behave as inconspicuously as possible because the huge monk population had a reputation for dislike of foreigners. Sir Charles Bell found that in 1921, and Ernst Schäfer and his party suffered from it, by their own rashness, in 1939.

Over the years our circle of friends among lamas and monks as well as laymen continued to widen, helped greatly by the work of the doctors at the hospital of the British Mission at Dekyilingka; we visited and were always warmly received at monasteries, large and small in many parts of central Tibet; and on my walks alone in the countryside I was sometimes engaged in conversation by monks who took me for one of my staff — for no Tibetan official was ever seen in public except on horseback attended by several mounted servants. They used to enquire amiably about what went on at our Mission. Perhaps the monastic community gradually came to accept our presence with less suspicion.

The following description of the ceremonies is based, therefore, on what I saw on several occasions, on what many Tibetan friends, monk and lay, have told me, and on written accounts in Tibetan by Thupten Sangay and Shankhawa Gyurme Sonam Tobgye. I have also referred to the works of some of the foreign writers mentioned above. In the ceremonies there was so much movement, so many people in so many different dresses took part that my description is inevitably deficient in some respects and inaccurate in others. That is something which I hope the sadly diminishing number of Tibetans who saw them before 1950 may correct and reinterpret.

The events are recorded as taking place in months according to the Tibetan calendar, so it is desirable to give a brief account of their system. The Tibetan year contains twelve lunar months, each of thirty days which necessitates the insertion of an intercalary month every three years to keep in line with the solar year. Thus the Tibetan first month, which was probably fixed to accord with farming activities, may fall any time between February and March of the western calendar. In each month the first, eighth and fifteenth days are specially devoted to religious observance. Certain dates which are deemed inauspicious may be omitted and replaced by the duplication of others.

The earliest dating system in Tibet was a cycle of twelve years, known as the lokhor, each designated by the name of an animal in the following order: mouse, ox, tiger, hare, dragon, snake, horse, sheep, monkey, bird, dog and pig. It is still in popular use; but from 1027 A.D. a sixty-year cycle known as rabchung ("completed") or lokham ("year-element") was introduced in which to each animal was assigned one of five elements (kham) — fire, water, earth, iron and wood, in that order. Each element covers two animal years in succession, one designated as male, the next female. The sixty-year cycle begins with the Fire-Female-Hare year.

How to represent Tibetan words and names is always a difficulty. Tibetan orthography is a complicated business for those who are unfamiliar with it. To give only two examples: what appears in the text as "Lama Losar" (The Priest's New Year) is properly Bla-ma Lo-gsar, and "lü" (ransom) is glud. On the advice and with the help of my editor, Michael Aris, an experienced Tibetan scholar, we have settled on a phonetic form throughout but have given the Tibetan orthography in a glossary which serves also as an index. No phonetic form satisfies everyone and there are inconsistencies in the one adopted but it is hoped that it will be intelligible.

Finally I must say how grateful I am to all who have helped in different stages of this book: the late Zurkhang Shappé, Wangchen Gelek, the most generous and wisest of my informants; Nick and Sophie Hole who reduced my turgid typescript to order and put it on a disk; Patrick Booz who completed most of the photo research; and two good friends, my editor Michael Aris for his meticulous scrutiny of the text which has saved it from many mistakes and infelicities — such as remain are due solely to me — and my patient publisher Anthony Aris for his constant encouragement and for his discrimination and hard work in tracing the best illustrations which give life to the book.

St. Andrews
February 1993

The Potala Palace seen from the Chakpori medical college.

The First Month

First Day: The Priest's New Year

བླ་མ་ལོ་གསར།

Before the celebration of the New Year could take place the accumulated evils of the past had to be driven out. That was done in a day-long dance ritual performed by masked monks in the eastern courtyard of the Potala, the Deyang Shar. It will be described in its proper place at the end of the year. The ceremonies of what is generally called the Gyetön, "The Happy Celebration" of the New Year, begin with receptions in the Potala by the Dalai Lama known respectively as the Lama Losar, the Priest's New Year, and the Gyalpo Losar, the King's New Year, reflecting the position of the Dalai Lama as *Chösi Nyiden*, "master jointly and severally of Church and State". It was deemed auspicious that every important event should take place in the first half of a lunar month in the morning while the sun is in the ascendant. The ceremony of the first day fulfilled those conditions completely.

Early in the morning, well before dawn, the Dalai Lama would be awakened to the sound of the ceremonial drum-roll peculiar to himself. After private prayer he would be offered auspicious wheat-flour, tea and rice and would receive white scarves from his teachers and personal attendants to whom he would give his blessing. After a short reception for high officials at which there were prayers and ritual offerings to the protectress deity of the Gelukpa sect, Penden Magzorma, the Dalai Lama would take his seat on a throne on the roof of the Potala where he would receive scarves and give his blessing to the whole body of officials. Tea, rice and meat were served. This part of the ceremony was not one to which foreign representatives were invited—fortunately perhaps because it was described as being piercingly cold in the chilly wind of a winter morning.

After a short pause the Dalai Lama would go in a formal procession to the great hall on the second floor of the Potala known as Sishi Puntsog, "The accumulation of blessings for a peaceful existence", for the main ceremony of the Lama Losar.

On the occasion of Sir Basil Gould's visit to Lhasa in 1936 his Mission was invited on this day. Through the anxiety of our guide that we should not commit a breach of etiquette by arriving late we were conducted to the Potala well before daylight. We waited at first in a dark cold passage and then in the hall itself where the abbots of the great monasteries, incarnate lamas and many monk dignitaries were assembled together with the body of lay officials. It was dimly lit and so cold that water in the offering bowls on the altars was frozen solid.

On the north side of the hall was the high golden throne of the Dalai Lama. On its right hand, seated on cushions, were rows of abbots, incarnate lamas and other monks, many in magnificent cloaks of red or yellow embroidered, with religious symbols, over their monastic dress. Opposite the throne, across the hall, also on cushions whose height was prescribed according to rank, were the lay officials. The highest of them wore the dress ordained for the day called "the Khalkha style", — heavy gold brocade ornamented with dragons, collar and cuffs of sable and a broad, flat, round hat with a fur brim, red silk top surmounted by a gold and turquoise ornament. Others wore the *gyaluché*, "Royal Dress", a short brocade jacket with a thick rainbow-coloured scarf over the left shoulder, and a pleated black silk skirt; on their heads was a small white cockleshell hat. We were seated on the left of the throne, on cushion seats according to rank, the Political Officer's being slightly higher than mine, and so on. We sat there for some time in considerable discomfort from the cold and from the inadequate protection of formal dress, and with legs discreetly crossed beneath us.

At last, from the passage leading to the hall came the shrilling of oboes and the glow of flickering lights. A long strip of white silk decorated with auspicious symbols was unrolled up to the throne and the Lord Chamberlain and assistants arranged the Dalai Lama's robes on the throne symbolizing his continued presence, though the new incarnation had not yet been discovered. The Regent and Prime Minister entered in procession, preceded by torch-bearers and musicians and surrounded by a cloud of incense. They prostrated themselves three times before the throne and took their places on lower thrones to the right of the Dalai Lama's, on which each laid a scarf. Then the abbots and lay officials came forward in order of precedence to make their prostration and offer scarves to the Dalai Lama's throne and to the Regent and Prime Minister. We also went in our turn to offer scarves and receive from the Lord Chamberlain a small strip of blue silk round our necks.

When everyone was seated again the Lord Chamberlain went round enquiring after the health of the guests on behalf of the Dalai Lama, to which all bowed in polite acknowledgement. Tea and rice were then served. The tea for the Dalai Lama was poured from a large golden teapot and was ceremonially tasted by a monk official on bended knee before being offered to the empty throne. For others the tea was poured from great silver pots.

Two learned Geshés then took up positions to the side of the throne and began a profound debate. One being questioned sat on the ground quietly answering points made by the challenger who gestured fiercely, stamping on the ground and stretching out an arm with his rosary hanging from it; sometimes he clapped his hands and uttered a high shout. After a while the positions were reversed and the challenger became the challenged. The manner of the debate follows quite closely that which is said to have been performed in Buddhist colleges in India in ancient times. Our lay friends told us that they were unable to follow the argument but no doubt it was heard with attention by the religious dignitaries. Meanwhile two monks — the Tretröpa — seated on either side of the hall were intoning what were described as auspicious verses about important events of the past.

Tea was served again and the debaters broke off their discussion for a time while the Dalai Lama's troupe of dancing boys, the Gartrupa, came in. There were thirteen of them, wearing light-coloured flowered silk robes with a girdle round the waist, and round flat brocade caps in shape rather like those worn in Hunza. They carried small axes painted green to resemble jade. They performed a stylized dance, brandishing their axes and striking angular postures, or occasionally making short leaps. The dance was accompanied by rather hollow sounding drums called *dama* and pipes known as *suna* said to be of Indian origin and possibly a Tibetan version of surnai. The troupe is recruited as a form of taxation from various villages which receive remission of taxes on that account. When the boys get too old they are given duties at the government office in the Shö. Similar dances are recorded in other parts of Tibet and in Ladakh and also resemble old Chinese ritual performances. The Fifth Dalai Lama, to whom much of the New Year ceremonial is attributed, is said to have organized the Lhasa troupe on the lines of similar dances in Ladakh.

After the dance, which is quite short, the debate is resumed. Rice is served and pieces of mutton are distributed, the particular section and size of each portion being regulated according to rank. We were rather bewildered about what to do with these gobbets but were rescued by our orderlies who bobbed up from behind with cloths to wrap them in and were later very pleased to be allowed to keep these highly prized presents. Another dance followed.

There follows a remarkable spectacle. Servants come in carrying a great assortment of food — baskets of Tibetan pastries, bread, dried fruits, sweets, joints of mutton and whole carcasses of sheep and yaks. Officials from various departments, headed by two Shappés (Cabinet Ministers) supervise the arrangement of all these things in a great heap on low stools in the centre of the hall, and appear to check lists of the presents which are handed to them. The Lord Chamberlain asks the Dalai Lama's permission to distribute the food; a handful of dried fruits and sweets is taken to all the guests; and then at a sign, a horde of servants rush in, and set about grabbing all they can from the heap. Some drag away the carcasses, others stuff pastries and fruit into the folds of their cloaks. Monks with long sticks are standing by and from time to time beat some of the mob who seem too violent, but it is done in a light-hearted way. When the floor has been cleared and calm restored the dancing boys perform again. Tea is served for the last time. Finally one of the Geshés who has been taking part in the debate recites a long prayer for good fortune. The two debaters are given special blue silk scarves. Then one of the Dalai Lama's monk bodyguards shouts to the assembly that the ceremony is over. The Dalai Lama, Regent and Prime Minister go off in procession; the high officials follow to escort him to his room at the top of the Potala; and we return home.

The rest of the day was given up to family celebrations, and we began a series of calls, with New Year presents, upon high officials and friends which was to last for several days. In every house the altar was specially decorated. There would be a wooden tray with two compartments, one for wheat flour and one for grains of barley; a silver bowl of *chang* (barley beer); *torma* —conical cakes of *tsampa* and butter; a sheep's skull decorated with coloured butter; a vase containing green barley sprouts, paper flowers and so on. Scarves would be exchanged and the tray of wheat flour and barley would be offered for a ritual pinch to be flicked in the air; then a sip of *chang* followed by tea and special food of the season — a rather solid cake of *tsampa* and butter, black truffles, sometimes a bowl of raw meat in a sauce of blood, sausages and a bowl of noodles. Fortunately, only a small amount had to be tasted before going on to the next house for the same reception.

2nd Day: The King's New Year

རྒྱལ་པོ་ལོ་གསར།

Up to the arrival of the Fourteenth Dalai Lama in 1939 members of the British Mission were invited on the first day. When I returned to Lhasa in 1946 I found that our invitation had been changed to the second day, the King's New Year, perhaps because we were seen as political rather than religious representatives. So I was able to see both occasions.

The ceremony of the second day followed the general pattern of that on the first but there were significant differences emphasizing the tradition of long-standing temporal sovereignty.

After a brief reception for his household in his rooms at the Potala, the Dalai Lama went, at a much later hour than on the previous day, in procession to the great audience hall. The abbots and incarnate lamas were not present; on this day only, all the lay officials wore the *gyaluché*, held to be the dress of the old royal princes. And accompanying the Dalai Lama's procession were thirteen officials in special dress reputed to resemble that worn in the time of the ancient kingdom of the seventh to ninth centuries A.D. They were arrayed in robes of precious old brocade

Opposite: *Official in the gyaluché dress.*

or flowered silk and had small conical yellow silk caps on their heads except for one who had a tall wide-brimmed hat in Mongolian style, topped by a peacock's feather. The leaders wore ornaments of unusual size — great circular golden, turquoise-studded charm boxes, a heavy turquoise pendant earring in the right ear and in the other a long golden bar, covered in slabs of turquoise, which reached down to the waist and had to be held in the hand. There were also necklaces of large coral beads and one of huge amber beads, some as big as a golf ball. I was told that about twenty other less elaborate robes were also worn on this day but only the principal figures take part in the ceremony at the Potala. These precious possessions were seized by the Fifth Dalai Lama from the palace at Nedong, of the effete Phamodru family. They are known as the *ringyen*, "the Ancient Ornaments", and are kept in the Potala treasury. A member of the Kashag, the cabinet, supervises the taking out and return when a meticulous check is made to see that not the smallest stone is missing.

Officials (below and opposite) wearing the ringyen ("Ancient Ornaments") during the King's New Year.

When the Dalai Lama is seated on his throne, a prayer is chanted to the accompaniment of oboes and cymbals, and the leaders of the Ringyenpa, the lay

officials authorized to wear the *ringyen*, offer him the Eight Auspicious Signs — the wheel of the dharma, conch, umbrella, banner of victory, golden fish, lotus, vase, and the *pelki be'u*, an intricate knot symbolizing compassion; the Eight Auspicious Objects — mirror, the *giwang* (a lump found in the neck of an elephant), curds, *kusha* grass, an *arura* (myrobalan), a white turnip and a red powder called *litri*; and the Seven Insignia of Royalty — sword, robes, boots, earring, fly whisk, elephant tusks, and the wish-fulfilling gem.

The assembly then perform their prostrations and present scarves. The Lord Chamberlain goes round to enquire after the health of the guests. Tea is offered by the leader of the Ringyenpa, and tea and rice are taken to the guests. The Dalai Lama's dancing boys perform their first dance. Two lamas of lower rank than on the first day begin their debate during which representatives from the Sakya and Kargyüpa monasteries make offerings to the Dalai Lama, as do officials who have been given new appointments. There follows an unusual and very interesting dance by a party from the estates of Drebuling, near Tsethang. They wear masks representing different deities and spirits who appeared to the Fifth Dalai Lama in a dream.

They included the benevolent figures of Tshangpa, Gyachin and Namtösé (Brahma, Indra and Vaishravana); Chenmizang the Guardian King of the West, the mountain deity Chamo Zangmo, several *driza* "perfume eaters" playing flutes, woodwinds and drums; Nöjin demons; Trülbum charnelhouse ghosts; *mi* and *mimayin*, humans and non-humans; a garuda and a peacock. They danced slowly and solemnly, singing softly to the accompaniment of a gentle, meandering, mysterious tune from flutes, muted woodwind, low-pitched drums and cymbals played by other members of the party. The music was quite unlike any other that I had heard in Tibet and was almost western in nature, reminiscent at times of Debussy. I later asked to be allowed to record the delightful dances and music at our Mission but was politely refused as it was so holy, and permission could not be given while the Dalai Lama was a minor. Similar dances were performed at the Karmapa's court in the fifteenth century.

Tea and rice were again served and the Dalai Lama's dancing boys performed another dance, this time more vigorous than on the first day and they carried swords instead of axes. They were accompanied by flutes and drums. Offerings to the Dalai Lama were brought in and piled up in the centre of the floor as on the first day. This time no meat was served to the officials but food was brought for them in napkins from their own houses and placed on low tables in front of them. The scramble for the heap of foodstuffs took place as before. Tea was served again and the dancing boys performed their last, vigorous, dance and concluded by chanting a short prayer. The debating lamas intoned a prayer of good fortune and received their scarves. The assembled guests rose to signify their thanks to the Dalai Lama and he withdrew in procession. By the time I attended the King's New Year he was about eleven years old and I was surprised to see that he tottered along with shaky steps supported by the Regent and Lord Chamberlain. I was told that this gait represented the Buddha as a child taking his first steps.

Opposite: *Crowd at the foot of the Potala watching the "sky-dancing rope game" during the King's New Year.*

After the ceremony the lay officials left the Potala by the wide, steep and slippery stone stairway on the south-east. They were preceded by servants dragging what appeared to be a stuffed yak down the steps to clear the way. At the foot of the Potala

a large crowd had gathered to watch what is described as Namdrotagtse, "sky-dancing rope game", or Chakhen Tagshur, "sliding down a rope like a bird". A man climbs up a rope to the top of a tall wooden mast and after standing precariously on a small platform, lies down on it and makes it revolve slowly. Finally he slides down the rope which has been fixed a short distance away from the base of the mast. Formerly the descent was down a long rope stretched diagonally from the masthead to a stone pillar some eighty yards away. Sir Charles Bell saw this done in 1921 but it was discontinued soon after because a man had fallen to his death. Such accidents appear to have been not infrequent and may have been quite numerous in still earlier times when, according to Kishen Singh ("Pundit A.K.") of the Survey of India, men slid down a rope from one of the lowest turrets of the Potala. The performers are from villages in Tsang on whom the duty is said to have been imposed by the Fifth Dalai Lama as a form of retribution for the opposition by the ruler and people of Tsang to his seizure of power in 1642. There is a saying that the mothers of the rope-sliders do not die from illness but from sorrow when their sons are taken. A variant of the saying attributing it to the mothers at Chongye suggests that there was a similar practice at one time in the Yarlung valley. It was also seen by Sarat Chandra Das at Shigatse where a man slid from the roof of the *dzong* some three hundred feet to the ground. The Abbés Huc and Gabet knew of it and called it "the dance of the spirits".

The custom, which appears to have originally been a form of human sacrifice, is recorded over two centuries from many places in the cis-Himalayan region by William Moorcroft, Capt. A. Gerrard, G.W.Traill, Lee Shuttleworth and others. It is generally described as a Vaishnavite ceremony, and the death of a human victim or an animal substitute is regularly mentioned. In 1981 the Hon. Penelope Betjeman attended two such ceremonies in the Sutlej valley and has described them in detail in *Saras: Bulletin of Asian Religious Art Series*, 1984 in which she gives references to earlier accounts.

3rd Day: Preparations for the Great Prayer

སྨོན་ལམ་ཆེན་མོའི་གྲ་སྒྲིག།

This day is taken up with preparation for the Mönlam Chenmo, the Great Prayer, which is to follow. This ceremony of great spiritual significance for all Tibet was introduced on a considerably smaller scale, in 1409 by the great reforming lama Tsongkhapa.

In the morning the monk officials and other religious dignitaries attend on the Dalai Lama in the Potala where an offering of incense is made to Penden Lhamo, the protectress deity of the Gelukpa sect. Then in the presence of the deity a ritual of divination by dough balls is performed to ascertain omens for the future prosperity of the Dalai Lama, the religion and the state and of all sentient beings. From this the day is sometimes called Tsesum Zendri, the "Rolling of Dough Balls on the Third Day".

A great prayer mast, the Ganden Darchen, is erected near the north-east corner of the Barkor. This task is, rather surprisingly, imposed on the *ragyapa*, the cutters-up of dead bodies. The Mipön, City Magistrates, go to report to the Dalai Lama that the mast has been erected. Meanwhile, two representatives of the Shengo, the Proctors, of Drepung were admitted and received instructions from the Lord Chamberlain regarding the conduct of the Mönlam Chenmo.

The Shengo, proctors of the Drepung monastery, carrying their heavy silver maces.

Later in the day virtually the whole of the official body, monk and lay, headed by the Regent went to the Nechung monastery to consult the State Oracle. There was a special dance in the courtyard of the monastery by the monks of Nechung in various masks. Then the Oracle appeared in a trance, made his pronouncement into the ear of the Regent and received scarves from the officials. Everyone then rode back to Lhasa where the lay officials went to a summer house in an open space to the north of the Potala where they had a lunch party with plenty of *chang* and also singing and dancing from the Dalai Lama's dancing boys. Then followed an archery contest; first a competition in shooting the longest distance, and then shooting at a target with whistling arrows, a last fling of the New Year.

Earlier in the day the two Shengo had arrived at Lhasa accompanied by their retinue including a body of *dobdob* monastic police, stalwart monks carrying long poles and whips, with their cheeks blackened, bobbed hair, and a red ribbon round their muscular right arms. The Shengo go to a room inside the approaches to the Jokhang and send their deputies to the office of the City Magistrates to demand that authority be handed over to them. The Magistrates withdraw behind closed doors after their attendants have thrown down their whips of office outside. The deputies then go to wells at different parts of the city and order them to produce adequate supplies of water. Later in the afternoon, members of the Kashag come to the courtyard of the Tsuklakhang to see the monks who have begun to arrive and to hear the Shengo read the document entrusting them with supervision of the city during the Mönlam Chenmo.

Thereafter their rule of iron, backed up by their fierce monk police, descends on Lhasa. Fines are imposed if the outside of anyone's house is considered dirty, if anyone uses bells on a horse or mule, if a woman appears outside without her headdress, if anyone is seen wearing ornaments or foreign shoes, or if there is any singing or disorderly behaviour, and on many minor peccadilloes, and shopkeepers and traders have to pay a tax if they want to carry on their business. It is said that these draconian measures bring in much profit to the Shengo during the twenty-one days of their tenure of office.

4th Day: Start of the Great Prayer

སྨོན་ལམ་ཆེན་མོའི་འགོ་བཙུགས།

From early morning monks from Drepung, Sera and Ganden and from other monasteries stream into Lhasa to take part in the Great Prayer. They hope to secure a seat in the Jokhang and somewhere to stay at night. Their number is generally estimated at twenty thousand. It is often implied that they all crowd into the Jokhang, but it seems impossible that the Khyamra Chenpo, the main prayer hall, and the Shingra, a courtyard in the south-western part of the Tsuklakhang complex could hold more than four or five thousand at most. The account by Thupten Sangay makes it clear that many have to find places not only in passages in the

Opposite: *A monk policeman* (dobdob).

Overleaf: *Monks outside the Tsuklakhang during the Great Prayer.*

Jokhang but also in the courtyard at the entrance to the Jokhang, in the Sungchöra to the south and in the Barkor surrounding the building. Those who find a place inside the Jokhang are permitted by the Shengo's officers to occupy it every day. On this and other occasions during the Great Prayer the power of the Shengo might be needed to restrain traditional rivalries between monks of different monasteries or colleges. Although they themselves were from Drepung, in punishing such quarrels the Shengo had a reputation for complete impartiality.

As for finding somewhere to stay, a few colleges had houses or rooms of their own but most monks would go to temples around the city or to shops, and many would be received in private houses as an act of special merit at this time.

6th Day: The Great Prayer

སྨོན་ལམ་ཆེན་མོའི་དངོས་གཞི།

Although an abbreviated prayer service and distribution of tea and food took place on the previous day, the regular day-long sessions began on the fifth day. There were three main prayer services, two of about three hours each from before dawn to midday and another in the afternoon. At one service, the Tri Rinpoché of Ganden preached a sermon; there were also short debates; and occasionally in the afternoon a longer debate between candidates for high religious degrees. At the two morning sessions, known as the *löntsok*, "wet assemblies", tea, rice and meat were served; and at the afternoon service, known as the *kamtsok*, "dry assemblies", only tea was provided. In the afternoon presents of money were distributed.

The expenses of all this were basically the responsibility of the government, but there were also large endowments, some dating back to the Manchu emperors of China; one from a wealthy former Khampa chieftain, Andru Podrang; and many other presents from rich noblemen and traders. In 1946 twenty thousand monks were recorded as being present and cash to the value of six hundred thousand rupees was distributed.

The British Mission also made a regular donation, and on the appointed day our Sikkimese Assistant Political officer accompanied by a red-coated orderly went round the assembled monks in the Khyamra carrying a stick of incense, and a scarf for the presiding abbot. I watched the distribution from a balcony and was given a scarf by a representative of the abbot.

10th Day: The Gathering of the Skygoers

མཁའ་འགྲོ་འདུ་བའི་དུས་ཚེས།

Thupten Sangay records a ceremony called Khandro Duwé Tütsé, "The Time for the Gathering of the Skygoers", when, after the first prayer session, high officials, monks and laymen go to the Meru temple, with which the Nechung State Oracle is connected, and there offer incense to him in his form as Öden Karpo, the chief of the *dralha*, the fierce protectors of the faith, and to hear his predictions. I am not clear how this is related to the *khandroma* — minor female deities of the sky.

15th Day: The Festival of the Great Miracle and the Offerings of the Fifteenth

ཆོ་འཕྲུལ་དུས་ཆེན་དང་བཅོ་ལྔ་མཆོད་པ།

This day, the Chotrü Tüchen, is the very heart of the Mönlam Chenmo, which is sometimes called the Chotrü Mönlam Chenmo. It commemorates the Great Miracle at Sravasti when the Buddha defeated the heretics and preached the dharma. The Dalai Lama attends the morning assembly in the Khyamra Chenpo of the Tsuklakhang where he leads a service of confession. Then he goes in procession to a throne on a dais outside the southern facade of the Jokhang and preaches on the Great Miracle to a great congregation of monks sitting in the wide open square. At the end of the sermon the Nechung Oracle presents the Dalai Lama with a scarf. The Dalai Lama and monks return to the Jokhang where a final service of prayers and chanting takes place.

In the evening there is a spectacular festival known as the Chönga Chöpa, the "Offerings of the Fifteenth". All afternoon monks and servants of the government, the great monasteries and noble houses have been busy all round the Barkor, erecting tall wooden scaffoldings often higher than the roof of the Tsuklakhang and neighbouring houses. On these they fix pyramidal leather frames covered with elaborate decorations in coloured butter — deities, lamas, demons, lions, dragons, garudas, auspicious signs, flowers, and more besides. Some of them incorporate movable figures; an oracle being the most popular. The shape of these huge *chöpas* resemble that of the *torma*, cake-offerings made of dough and butter or of painted wood seen on most altars. The ingenuity and skill in the craftsmanship is remarkable and there is keen competition to produce the best *chöpa*.

When night falls they are all brightly lit up by countless butter-lamps, torches and Japanese-style lanterns or recently by the less attractive light of pressure lamps. Soon the Dalai Lama's regimental escort marches in, headed by their band; and after a while the drums and fifes of the dancing boys herald the arrival of the Dalai Lama in his carrying chair, attended by a large body of officials and surrounded by torch-bearers. He gets out of the chair and walks round to inspect the whole display. In front of each *chöpa* the donor sits on a chair and, of course, rises and bows deeply when the Dalai Lama approaches. At the end of his circuit the Dalai Lama decides which *chöpa* deserves the first prize and soon after departs in procession.

All this time a huge crowd has lined the street, kept back by ropes manned by the troops and the Shengo's police. After the procession has left, the ropes are removed and the crowd surges forward laughing and singing to swarm round the Barkor, admiring the great *chöpas*. Surprisingly, no one seems to get hurt in the rush. We used to watch the Dalai Lama's visit from a friend's house opposite the entrance

Setting up scaffolding outside the Tsuklakhang for the chöpa, butter offerings, on the 15th day of the 1st month.

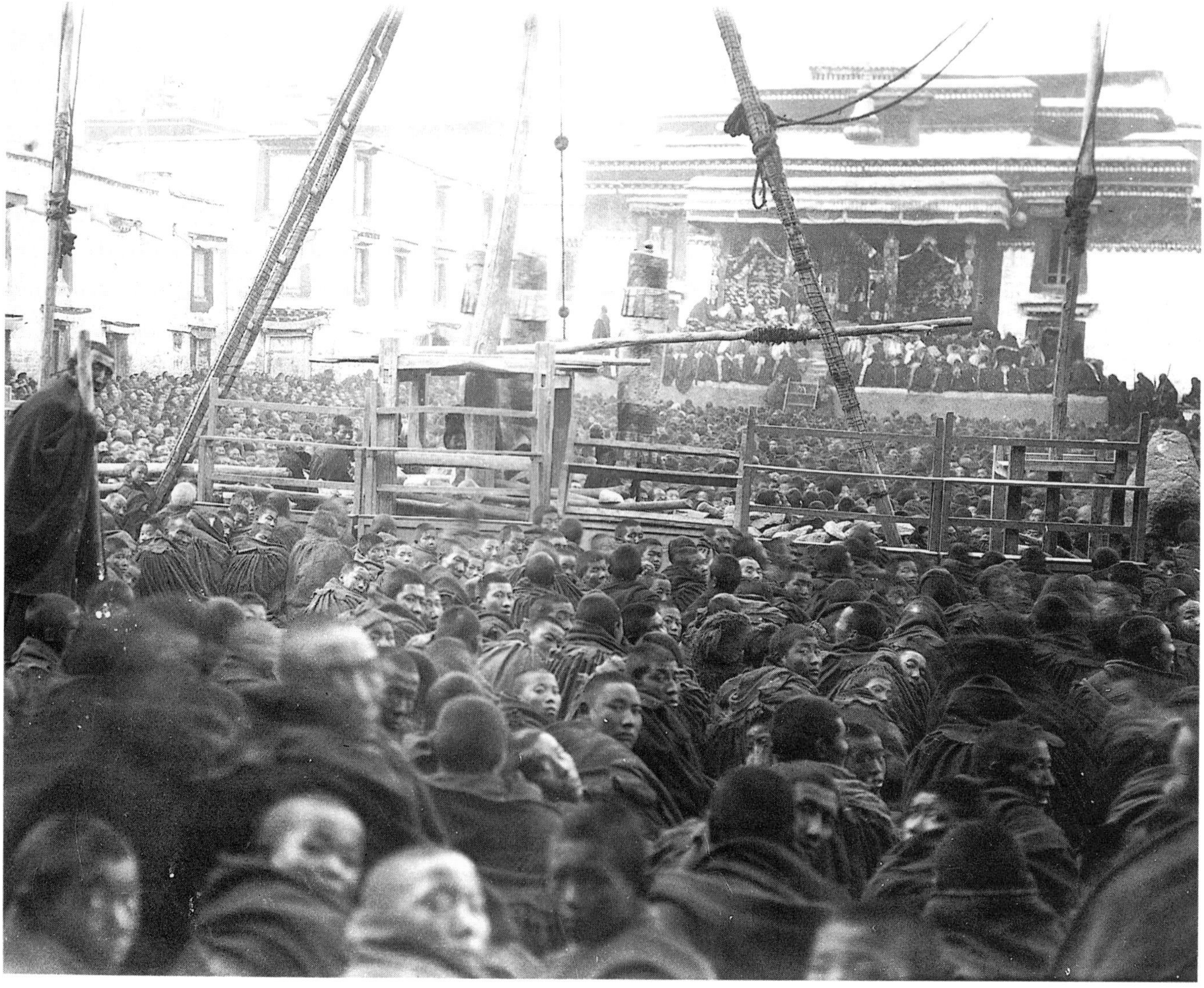

The display of butter offerings.

to the Jokhang; and after he had left we went down into the crowd to make the circuit ourselves. The Shengo provided us with a bodyguard of brawny *dobdob* monks to help us along; but it was an occasion of great good humour, exuberance and forbearance. After our visit we usually rode home but one evening we went back with our guard to our friend's house where we were all given tea. It was a pleasure to see our fierce-looking monks with their blackened faces behaving with the quiet good manners typical of all Tibetans.

During this evening festival the ordinary monks were not allowed to enter the Barkor and in the release from the stern discipline of the previous days the crowd of lay men and women kept up their merriment all night singing the songs of their different villages and districts, exchanging verses and capping what the others had said in a form known as *tshikgya*. Competitions of that sort might be kept up on the following day with people of neighbouring villages advancing to a middle point to exchange verses and pithy sayings. But at Lhasa, by daybreak the great *chöpas* had to be dismantled and the butter stripped off. Poor people probably managed to secure a good deal but I understood that most of it was sold to tanners. The quantities involved were enormous and I was told of thirty loads of butter being used for one *chöpa*.

The fifteenth day appears as the high point in the Mönlam Chenmo for although it continued formally until the twenty-fifth of the month, concentration on the prayer sessions seems to have been relaxed to some extent and there were many other ceremonies, mostly of a lay character. Many ordinary monks began to drift back to their monasteries as the amount of the cash presents gradually declined.

16th Day: The Priest's Banquet

བླ་མ་དགའ་སྟོན།

On a chosen day between the sixteenth and eighteenth of the month the Kashag, the Tibetan cabinet, entertained the Tri Rinpoché of Ganden, the abbots of the great monasteries, the Shengo and other religious dignitaries who played a leading part in the Mönlam at a banquet (known as the Lama Gatön) in a room above the western entrance to the Jokhang known as the Khamsum Tsomchen.

19th Day: The Brilliant Invocation of the Glorious Goddess

དཔལ་ལྷའི་གཟབ་གསོལ།

On a chosen day between the nineteenth and the twenty-first the Dalai Lama presides over a service when incense is offered to the protectress deity Penden Lhamo, and confessional prayers are recited at the small chapel of the goddess in the turret at the south-eastern corner of the Jokhang roof. The ceremony is known as Pelhé Zabsö. All the high officials attend and after the ceremony the people of Lhasa in their best clothes and ornaments come in large numbers to offer incense.

From the twenty-second of the month the nature of the ceremonies undergoes a great change with three successive events of a military character introduced by the Fifth Dalai Lama in recognition of the services of the Mongol chieftain Gushri Khan in defeating his opponents and establishing him in power in 1642. Every feature reflects the Oirad Mongol influence.

22nd Day: Preparing the Camp at Lubu

ཀླུ་སྒུག་སྒར་སྒྲིག།

One of the Yaso commanders (George Tsarong) and attendants in ceremonial dress.

Early on the twenty-second a beautifully decorated tent in a small enclosure is set up on a grassy meadow across a small branch of the Kyichu south of the Lingkor, where it passes the boundary of the Shuktrilingka south-east of the Potala. This is to be the headquarters of two noble officials who have been appointed with the Mongol title of Yaso as commanders of two wings of the ancient militia to lead the military exercises of the next two days. In the morning, dressed in magnificent robes and mounted on ponies caparisoned with gilded trappings and coloured rosettes on their heads, the Yaso ride in procession with a large retinue to the Jokhang where on the terrace at the entrance porch they are met by the monastic proctors, *gekö*, of Drepung— known as the Shengo — who give them instructions regarding their responsibilities during the ceremonies. They are also received by a member of the Kashag who gives them a written decree dating from the time of the Fifth Dalai Lama prescribing their duties, and adds his own exhortation about their proper performance. Then, after tying a white ceremonial scarf on to the Juya Darchen — the Mast of Good Policy — to the west of the Jokhang, they ride in state round the Barkor to Lubu where a crowd of their relations, friends and onlookers is waiting. The ceremony of the Lubu Gardrik ("Preparing the Camp at Lubu") follows.

The Yaso take their seat on thrones with low, carved and painted wooden tables in front and their attendants line up on either side. The Yaso robes are of the most costly brocade embroidered with dragons on the front and back, and so heavy they can stand up by themselves. They wear large, round, flat hats with a fur brim and red silk crown with a vase-shaped gold and turquoise ornament and a coral button on top. The robe is girded by a wide gold belt and they wear a dagger, an embroidered purse and a silk-covered cup case. Their attendants are also in fine brocade or silk of blue or green; some have a long red baldric over the right shoulder; some have flat fur-brimmed hats; others have Mongol style fez-shaped brocade hats; they wear gold bracelets and carry coral rosaries. The retinue is completed by a group of six ladies. Two are maids of honour, usually relations of the Yaso; two are servers of *chang* (barley beer) and are also of noble rank. These four are dressed in fine brocade with the traditional bright striped apron, and a lavish display of ornaments of turquoise, gold, pearls, coral and amber. Their horn-shaped headdresses are decorated with large balls of coral. The other two are household servants and are less richly dressed.

The maids of honour present a silver bowl of *chang* to the Yaso who ritually flick a few drops into the air. The senior Yaso then reads out the Fifth Dalai Lama's

The maids of honour of the Yaso commanders.

decree. After which the junior reads a proclamation about the proceedings and repeats the exhortation given by the Kashag.

The expense to the Yaso of their term of office is very heavy indeed. Different dress has to be worn on different occasions and although some items may be borrowed from friends, there is an element of competition to go one better than one's predecessor.

An account of the Yaso and their activities has been given by Joachim Karsten in the *Proceedings of the Csoma de Körös Symposium*, 1983.

The Yaso commanders (Ruthog Dapön) and attendants.

23rd Day: The Review at Trapchi

གྲྭ་ཕྱི་རྩིས་བཞེར།

Standard-bearer with one of the venerated banners known as the "Royal Father and Son, Life Force of the State".

Early in the morning the cavalry assemble at Lubu for the Trapchi Tsisher. It is the duty of the leading noble families, headed by the four Depön, to provide detachments of a fixed number of armed mounted men. They wear chain-mail, much of it mere remnants, steel breast plates, steel helmets with brocade lappets and peacock plumes, heavy cloth trousers decorated with blue devices, and special boots. Each has a flintlock gun or a modern rifle, a lance and a quiver of five plumed arrows. Formerly the ponies would have worn armour but only some pieces of that equipment survive in a few of the noble houses and it is no longer used.

The cavalry are joined by two stalwart standard-bearers wearing particularly fine armour with large steel breast-plates; they have special helmets on the frontlet of which the name of Allah is inscribed in gold filigree. It is unknown whether the helmets date from eighth-century contacts with the Arabs or from some other source and period, but the armour is greatly venerated under the name Shungsog Gyalpo Yapsé, "The Royal Father and Son, Life Force of the State". Each standard-bearer carries a tall lance wrapped in a painted banner and crowned with a trident, which are called the Tensung Marnak, the "Red and Black Protectors of the Faith", perhaps representing warriors from the retinue of Pehar or Penden Lhamo. They are said to be or to resemble the standards of Gushri Khan's forces.These precious objects are kept in the treasury of the Jokhang and a representative of each of the main offices of the government has to be present when they are taken out.

Meanwhile, open-fronted tents have been pitched near the Trapchi barracks on the sandy plain north of the city for the Kashag, other officials, the Yaso and guests; and kitchen tents for serving tea and food.

When the Yaso, who on this day wear a special dress known as "the Khalkha style", with a heavy fur collar and cuffs, have inspected the troops they send a message to the Kashag that they are about to start for the Trapchi plain. Then, each at the head of a wing and followed by the standard bearers, the Yaso lead their troops, numbering about five hundred, past the front of the Potala and through the north side of the city to the Trapchi plain where they take up their position some way north of the tents. The Yaso go to their own tent where they are offered *chang* by the maids of honour who have come in advance. The two standard-bearers are provided with seats on either side of a table of offerings opposite the Kashag's tent.

When the Kashag have arrived accompanied by all the lay officials, some in blue brocade, and have taken their seats, the Yaso approach and offer scarves. The standard-bearers accompany them and then return to their seats and take off their heavy helmets. The review, the Tsisher, is ready to begin.

Opposite: *Soldiery in old armour at the Trapchi*

An official from the Tsikhang where the state accounts and records are kept presents the Kashag with a list of the detachments of the right wing. There is a pause for tea and rice and then an officer asks permission for the review to begin. The first detachment, that of the senior Depön family of the Gabshi Doring, rides up in front of the Kashag, and the Tsikhang official steps up to the tent and bowing almost double as he sweeps off his hat, announces in a loud voice that the number of men and horses is correct. He is followed in succession by four boys, from the Tsikhang school for aspiring officials, smartly dressed in fine broadcloth with round yellow hats and their hair in neat pigtails down their backs. They come up in turn to the Kashag's tent and bowing deeply report in a shrill voice on different items of the equipment — so many saddles, guns, lances, arrows, pairs of boots and so on. The other detachments of the right wing — about twenty of them — follow and the same procedure is gone through. After that there is an interval for lunch; and then the tally of the left wing is presented and the review takes place in the same way.

When it is all over there is a wholesale distribution of scarves to the participants and a stack of packages is arranged in front of the Kashag's tent containing presents of silk, cloth and tea for the Yaso and other officials. Formerly this was the occasion for a lavish present of silver and silk from the Manchu Emperor of China, but after 1911 the distribution was made on behalf of the Dalai Lama. The Yaso and other officials offer thanks to the Kashag and the Yaso prostrate themselves in the direction of the Potala. The troops then circle back and pass in front of the Kashag before riding back to Lubu by way of the Lingkor.

Soldiery in old armour at the Trapchi Tsisher.

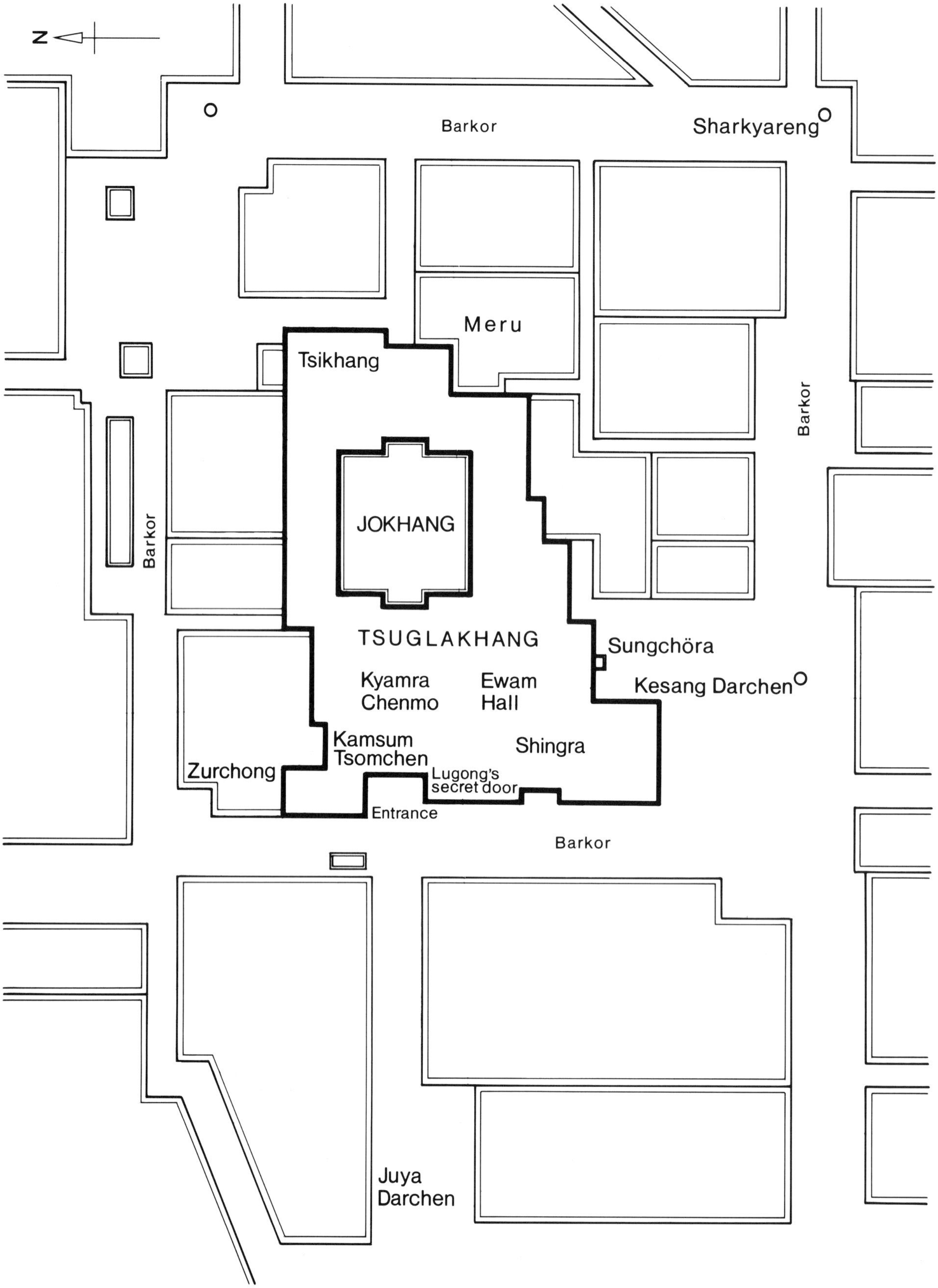

Plan of the Lhasa Jokhang and surrounding buildings
(with acknowledgement to Zasak Jigme Taring)

24th Day: Casting out the Votive Offering for the Great Prayer

སྨོན་ལམ་གཏོར་རྒྱག།

The ceremony of Mönlam Torgya is the longest and most spectacular event of the New Year celebrations. It is the high point of the Yaso's tenure of office and the day for which the Tsisher was the preparation. It brings together religious and secular elements and marks the formal end of the Mönlam Chenmo.

On this occasion the cavalry are joined by a band of foot soldiers called Zimchongpa. The orthography and even the meaning of the name are obscure. Nominally they number five hundred but I do not think there were more than two hundred when I saw the ceremony. The men are based in the Shö quarter below the Potala where some of them have houses; others live in neighbouring villages. They have specific duties throughout the year such as carrying banners in processions and pitching the Dalai Lama's Mongolian tent which is taken when he travels. For the Torgya ("Casting Out the Votive Offering") they are reinforced by others who are paid for the day. They are organized into two wings with the Mongol names of Julag and Shangso and are supposed to be descendants of Gushri Khan's infantry. They wear chain-mail, which is in very good condition compared with that of most of the cavalry, steel helmets with large plumes or a pair of flags like the headdress of some oracle priests; and they are variously armed with matchlocks, swords, bows and arrows; some carry large round shields of strongly made wickerwork; others have copper trumpets. They have their own sacred standard but I did not learn what warlike deity it represents. The commanders of the force are nominally the two *dapön* of the Ü province, a post that appeared to be virtually in abeyance; they are represented by two minor lay officials with two assistants, who are known as "officials for a month" and are allowed to wear the *gyaluché* dress to which they are not usually entitled. The effective commander is an experienced steward of the Shö who wears a helmet with his *gyaluché* dress instead of the little white hat. On the morning of the twenty-fourth the Zimchongpa assemble at the Shö to await their part in the proceedings.

The centre of activity is the forecourt of the Jokhang where it can be seen by the Dalai Lama from a window curtained with yellow silk in the Zurchong room to the north of the court. The Kashag watch from the verandah of the reception room, the Khamsum Tsomchen, over the porch of the Jokhang.

The ceremony begins with the arrival of the Shengos and their assistants who march from the Shingra gate, a little way south of the main entrance to the Jokhang. They are attended by their monk police headed by a brawny *dobdob*, called the Shangpo Shingnyer, carrying a huge wooden pole. They take their seats on a bench below the Dalai Lama's window. Some of the monks go back to the Shingra gate and throw down a bundle of rods and whips which are taken up by the attendants of the City Magistrates, signifying that control of the city has been handed back to the civil authorities.

Then an outburst of explosions and war cries announces the arrival of the Zimchongpa at the south-west corner of the Tsuklakhang where they wait while their leaders accompanied by the City Magistrates and their standard-bearers go forward to prostrate themselves towards the Dalai Lama's window. Then the

Two Shengo, proctors of Drepung.

Zimchongpa march noisily up to the forecourt of the Jokhang. Some line the Barkor while others form up in two files in the centre of the road. They take it in turn to display their martial prowess, singing war songs about Penden Lhamo as they do so. The bowmen brandish their bows and the swordsmen make a great show of fencing. Then those with firearms taunt the opposing rank, challenging them with abusive language much enjoyed by the onlookers. This is known as *bepa*, "incitement", which, I am told, sometimes ends in fighting behind the scenes. They hold their firearms waist-high pointing towards the opposing rank and after many theatrical gestures they loose them off simultaneously with much noise and smoke. Finally

The Shengo arrive at the forecourt of the Jokhang for the Mönlam Torgya.

The Yaso and retinue arrive for the Mönlam Torgya.

The Yaso prostrate themselves to the Dalai Lama, who may watch from an upper window overlooking the forecourt.

The Zimchongpa perform their "coiled snake" display at the Mönlam Torgya.

they trot off, one file in a zig-zag movement, the other running round in a circle until they form a compact mass, known as the coiling snake.

When the road is clear it is the turn of the cavalry who have in the meantime circled the city, each wing by a different route, meeting at the south-east corner of the Barkor. Thrones have been prepared there for the Yaso who are offered *chang* by the maids of honour and then are showered with scarves and presents by the general public who seek in this way to share in the Torgya. The Yaso then lead their troops to the south-west corner of the Barkor where they dismount and walk with their attendants to the forecourt of the Jokhang where they prostrate themselves to the Dalai Lama after which they walk back, mount their horses and lead the cavalry slowly past the Jokhang and on round the Barkor to the south-east corner again.

After a short pause four monks of the Namgye Tratsang — the Dalai Lama's special monastery in the Potala — wearing tall yellow hats like Roman helmets, and yellow silk waistcoats under their maroon robes, carry out two long silver horns and, facing west, blow a prolonged series of blasts. They move to the opposite side of the forecourt where they are joined by four more monks with two more silver horns and, facing the entrance to the Jokhang, they join in another summons. A long file of the Namgye Tratsang monks comes out from the Jokhang. There are about fifty of them; most carry large round drums with gilded frames and green backs supported on long handles and beaten with a single long, crooked drumstick. About ten others have small cymbals, *sinyen*, of a type used in rituals of exorcism. The monks, who are an élite community, are dressed in their best ceremonial clothes with brocade waistcoats and long pleated cloaks called *göber*, and a pendant on the back, *gyabdar*, hanging from a rectangular turquoise ornament. They take up position in the forecourt. The horns sound a long blast, the drums beat and the cymbal players turn towards the Jokhang entrance clashing their cymbals. A double line of laymen carrying tall cylindrical banners come out and after them the *torma*, in which all evil influences are stored, is brought out by a body of well-dressed laymen. It is a tall pyramidal structure with fretwork wings surmounted by a grinning skull mask with a spear and small umbrella on top. The standards and *torma* are taken off down the Barkor, and the Shengo who have been sitting near the Jokhang entrance quietly withdraw; their duties now are ended.

The Yaso's cavalry ride past the Jokhang.

A small party of monks wearing brightly coloured brocade shawls instead of the *göber* come into the forecourt. Like all Namgye Tratsang monks they are noticeably good-looking with shining clean faces and arms. Eight, carrying silver censers and two with silver ritual vessels, form two ranks facing each other. Their leader, the officiating priest, performs a hieratic dance between and around their ranks chanting a prayer of exorcism and gesturing solemnly with his bell and *dorje* while the monks around the court keep up a rhythmic accompaniment with drums and cymbals. Finally the officiant is handed a silver chalice containing a red-coloured ball of dough. An attendant monk pours holy water over it from a silver ewer and after an incantation the priest throws it out. This is done twice more after which the celebrants go back into the Jokhang and the other monks surrounding the square proceed down the Barkor, with drums beating and cymbals clashing, following the *torma* towards the south-west corner of Tsuklakhang. There they meet another *torma* carried in procession from the Sungchöra — the wide open court on the south side of the Jokhang — by monks from the Ngakpa college of Drepung who have been conducting a similar exorcism ceremony. They are renowned for their smart appearance and the devout manner of their attention to their duties.

When the procession from the Jokhang has left it is followed shortly by the Ganden Tri Rinpoché who comes out of the Jokhang wearing robes of maroon and

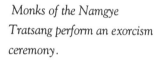

Monks of the Namgye Tratsang perform an exorcism ceremony.

yellow, and a yellow, peaked, monastic hat with a tasselled eyeshade. He is preceded by a file of monks with sticks of incense and followed by a large retinue of yellow-hatted Geshés with yellow shawls each carrying a maroon blanket in front of him. A yellow state umbrella is carried behind the Tri Rinpoché. Then there emerges from the Jokhang a long procession of the Nechung Oracle's *khor*, a sort of phantom bodyguard, about sixty of them in all. First a line of small boys wearing demon masks, then men in well-preserved chain-mail with round steel helmets, carrying flags on lances, then other men in armour with tall helmets, then some in monks' dress wearing large round red hats with a little crown, then a party of black-hat magicians, and finally a group in skull masks preceding a number of the Nechung monks in yellow hats carrying the Oracle's trident-headed standards.

The Tri Rinpoché of Ganden enters the Tsuklakhang.

A loud burst of oboes and cymbals and some hectic activity at the door of the Jokhang signal the appearance of the Oracle who rushes out in a state of possession grasping his sword and bow. After gyrating round the courtyard, he sets off down the Barkor supported by two stalwart monks, in pursuit of the *torma*. By now the two processions have combined and march off cheerfully to an open space south of the city near the former Chinese *yamen*. There the two *torma* have been put down and are surrounded by a heap of brushwood. As soon as the Oracle arrives he shoots an arrow at them. The pyre is set alight. The Oracle collapses and is taken off in his carrying chair to his Lhasa monastery of Meru. The Zimchongpa who have firearms loose off a deafening volley; the others brandish their weapons with defiant shouts. The cavalry ride round the fire with high-pitched war cries. Ritual weapons (*zor*) such as knives and spears are hurled into the blaze.

The Nechung Oracle comes to follow the torma.

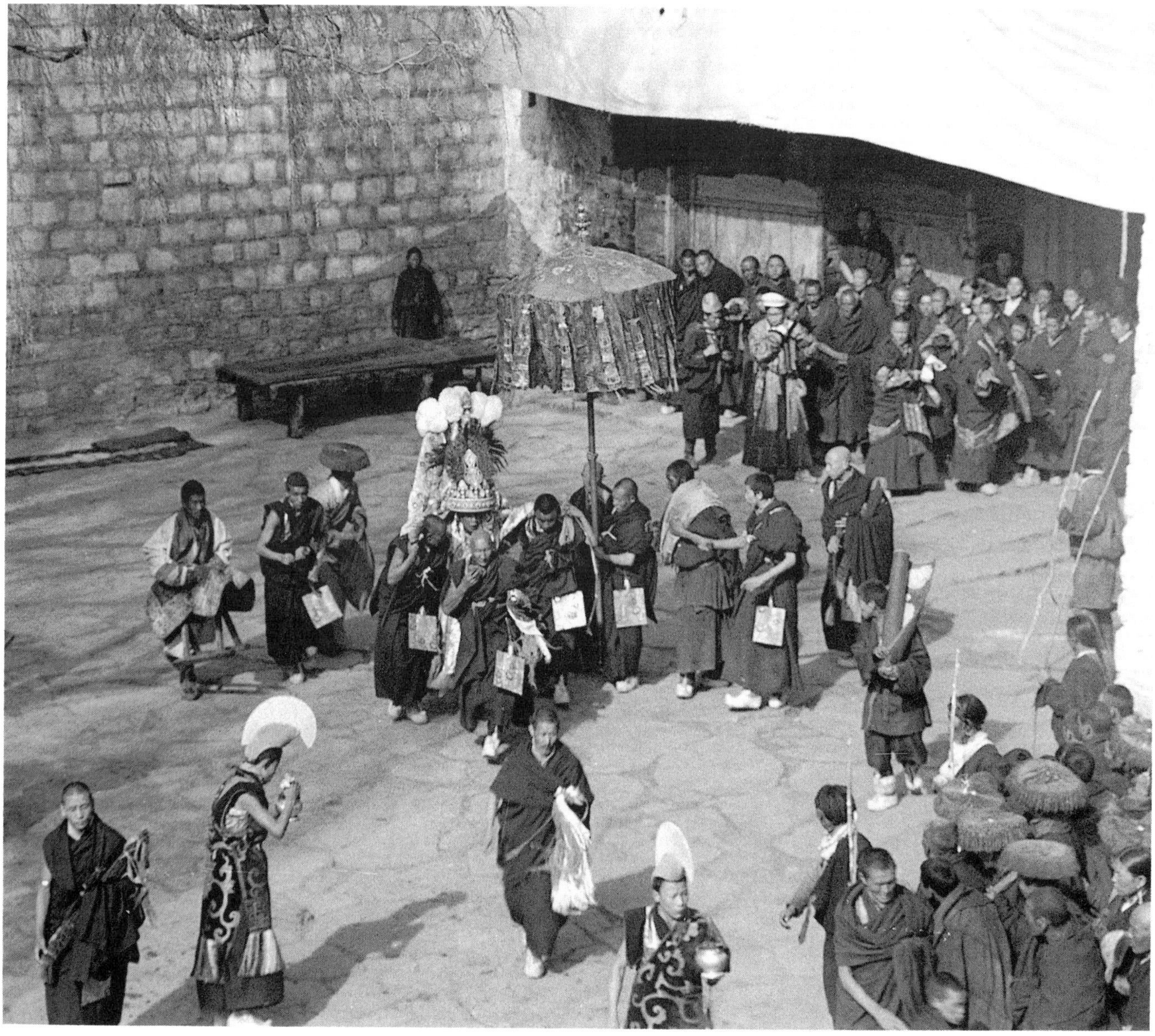

Meanwhile three ancient cannon have been primed. They are known as the Idiot, and the Old and Young She-demon; two of them appeared to have leather barrels bound with iron. They were brought from the Shö by the Zimchongpa some days before with a supply of powder and shot. They are aimed at a black tent on the side of a mountain across the Kyichu known as Chakya Karpori "The Mountain of White Bird Droppings," apparently from streaks of white on its slopes; but there are other forms of the name. I was told that there is a black sheep inside the tent and that two servants from the Shö have to hide on the hill to mark the effect of the shots. The cannon are fired some ten times with loud reports but on the occasions that I saw the shots all fell short or wide. The mountain is ill-omened by reason of a large heap of stones on its western end which is reputed to be the burial place of the apostate king Langdarma, and the cannonade is intended to ward off its evil influence on the city.

When the hubbub and excitement are over, the participants make their way back by way of the Juya Darchen, west of the Jokhang, to the forecourt where they make a farewell salutation to the Dalai Lama. The cavalry ride off round the town and back to Lubu. The Zimchongpa go off to the Shö. The monks of Namgye Tratsang and Drepung Ngakpa return to their monasteries except for the officiants in the exorcism ceremonies who are received at the Dalai Lama's audience in the late afternoon, where they are given scarves and rewards. This is also the occasion for the presentation of scarves and gifts to lamas and religious dignitaries who have acquired distinction during the Mönlam Chenmo. After the Torgya some of the monks who have come for the Mönlam may collect stones to reinforce the banks of the Kyichu east and south of the city as a symbolic gesture to avert a flood similar to the one which is said to have damaged the Jokhang many years ago.

The State Oracle of Nechung (the Nechung Chökyong) figures in many important ceremonies. The history of that institution and descriptions of many other oracles, deities and spirits are comprehensively covered in the classic work by the late René de Nebesky-Wojkowitz, *Oracles and Demons of Tibet*. I shall record only what I saw for myself.

When Sir Basil Gould visited Lhasa in 1936 the Nechung Oracle, to general surprise, came to visit him. Such a meeting had never happened before. He was a sturdy monk with a large, smiling, rather pale face and an open and cheerful manner who later became a very good and hospitable friend. He was about forty-two years old and his name was Lobzang Namgye. He had formally been a junior official in the Shö office, known to be sociable and very fond of mahjong. In 1934 without warning and much against his will he was chosen for the position and become a greatly venerated personage with the title of Ta Lama and the honorific epithet of Chöjé and the duties of a Chökyong, a protector of the faith, and the head of a small wealthy monastery with a pleasant sunny house of his own. During my time at Lhasa before his death in 1945, whenever I left or returned there officially, I would find his steward waiting by the side of the road with an urgent command to go up to Nechung for tea with the Ta Lama, which always included a delicious lunch. At other times I visited him in his country estate in the Tölung valley where he and his monks relaxed in a pleasant park, wearing holiday dress and enjoying archery at which the Oracle was expert. In return he came frequently to Dekyilingka often at short notice. In 1937 he invited me to attend a ceremony at Kundeling monastery where he went in the second month of each year to prophesy to Taktsa Rinpoché.

We were taken into a rather dark hall at the end of which stood a tall gilded chair for the Oracle. To its left side the lama was seated on a throne; on the other side the monks of Nechung with their prayer books and musical instruments; the rest of the hall apart from a central space was crowded with the monks of Kundeling. The Oracle's arrival at the monastery was greeted by the booming of long trumpets and he entered the hall to the shrilling of oboes. He was bareheaded, priestlike and in a long robe of gold brocade with a short cape and an apron with long tassels of rainbow colours. His boots were white with gold embroidery. Attendants carried his various accoutrements. To the gentle murmur of drums and cymbals he went to take his seat on the chair. A framework of gold bars with white plumes on top was strapped on his back, a large silver archer's ring was put on his thumb, and a large silver breast-plate with the sacred syllable HRI was hung round his neck. Each object was thoroughly censed, and smoke was wafted round the Oracle's head; the air was soon filled with heady fragrant fumes.

His monks then began in deep voices the first of three invocations to the deity. Meanwhile the Oracle sat with his feet wide apart and a drowsy look, shifting his position, moistening his lips and sometimes opening his eyes. The prayer ended in a crescendo of sound. When the second invocation began the great gold helmet, encrusted with jewels, with a mass of long black, drooping vulture feathers topped by white vulture plumes, was put on his head and firmly tied with red bands. It weighs about sixty pounds and can only be worn when he is in a trance. Its brocade wings were draped round his shoulders, a sword, which he grasped by the middle, was put into his right hand and a large, decorated bow in his left. Now he became uneasy and tremors passed through his body. He turned pale and sweat was wiped from his brow by his attendants. His hands grasping the sword and bow clenched and unclenched. All the time the deep chanting and the clouds of incense fumes heightened the almost hypnotic effect. After a short pause the third invocation began with increased intensity. Now "the god came down" — *lhabeb* — and as the spirit entered his body the Oracle's tremors became fiercer; his face turned scarlet; his mouth spread in a terrible grin; his eyes opened in a set stare; he drummed violently on the ground with his feet and his breath came in sharp hissing gasps. The convulsions became stronger and his body was filled with power that made him hurl himself forward and backward and twist to one side; he bent forward so violently that the great helmet almost touched the ground. It was astonishing that so seemingly unathletic a person could perform such contortions. His four attendants had to struggle to control him during these convulsions, during which the Taktsa Rinpoché threw handfuls of grain in front of him.

At last when it was perceived that the full possession of the deity was upon him he was released to leap into the centre of the hall where he danced wildly with stiff jerky steps circling the hall, with wide sweeps of his sword and bow from which the surrounding monks had to shrink back. Suddenly he rushed towards the Rinpoché and flung his arms around him. His attendants hurried after him and wrapped the folds of his helmet around the two. We could see the Oracle's shoulders heaving and from behind the screen came strangled, high-pitched sounds as he prophesied to the lama. His words were noted down by a principal monk who alone is able to interpret them. Then he was led back to his chair and the monks of Kundeling came to offer scarves and receive a strip of red silk round their necks. Once more he stood up and tottered towards the Rinpoché to whom he gave a scarf; a jade bowl of tea was put into his hands and after he had offered it to the lama, who sipped it, the contents were carefully poured into the cupped hands of the monks standing nearby — a much coveted benediction. Then still standing in front of the Rinpoché's throne he suddenly fell stiffly backwards. His attendants caught him just before he reached the floor. We were only about ten feet from him and watched as the helmet, sword, breast-plate and ring were taken from his rigid body. It had been disturbing, almost frightening, to watch my gentle friend being so horribly transformed, and it was a relief to see his body gradually relax, the dreadful rictus leave his face, and his head rest on the shoulder of an attendant as he was carried out of the hall.

He came in to Dekyilingka later in the morning, tired, and with the red mark of the great helmet still on his brow. It used to take several hours for him to recover, but as he got used to it, the time became less. He drank some tea but would eat nothing. When I said I had been troubled by the ceremony he laughed and asked if I had taken photographs as he wanted to see how he looked. I had not done so, out of respect, but on my next visit I tried, though rather unsuccessfully because the hall was so dark.

Later, I got several photographs of him at ceremonies out of doors. However the possession is induced, there was certainly no pretence about it. I saw other oracles entering that state and have heard and read about others in different parts of Tibet. The manner is everywhere the same though what different mediums do when possessed by the spirit may vary. Some twist swords and iron bars into knots, others hurl spears, and sometimes onlookers get hurt, even killed. If that happens the medium incurs reproof or some punishment from the Dalai Lama, for even though they are protectors of the faith they are still ultimately answerable to the Dalai Lama.

25th Day: The Invitation to Maitreya

བྱམས་པ་གདན་འདྲེན།

This ceremony, the Jampa Dendren, is in a very different mood from those of the preceding days. The air having been cleared of evil influences by the Mönlam Torgya, the time is propitious for an invitation to the Future Buddha, the kindly Jampa (Maitreya), to speed his coming.

Before daybreak the Kashag, Yaso, other high officials and many onlookers gather in front of the Jokhang around a flat cart decorated with silk hangings and artificial flowers. The moon in its last quarter sheds a pale glow on the white buildings and a chill wind blows from the east. At the first hint of dawn there is a clamour of music from inside the Jokhang and a party of monks in cloaks and yellow hats, carrying tall banners and silver censers, precede the Ganden Tri Rinpoché and his retinue of senior Geshés who are followed by the silver image of Jampa brought from its chapel in the Jokhang by reverent bearers. It is placed on a pedestal on the cart supported by several monks while others hold a number of ceremonial umbrellas — yellow, red, peacock-coloured — over its head. The Tri Rinpoché and the Umdze (Precentor) of the Mönlam assembly perform a short prayer service. The officials and onlookers heap scarves onto and around the image and then, preceded by monks of the Meru and Shidé monasteries carrying banners, incense and ritual vessels, the cart dragged by a large number of pullers begins its clockwise circuit of the Barkor with music all the way. The privilege of pulling the cart is shared, so I was told, by the craftsmen of Lhasa — carpenters, stone masons, metal workers and so forth — and a party of men from Markham in eastern Tibet; *dobdobs* — fighting monks — from Drepung are also allowed to volunteer their help. On the north side of the Barkor a large procession is waiting to lead the circuit. There are many banners, the Nechung Oracle's *khor*, effigies of a yak and an elephant and of two tall deities, one with a red face, the other blue.

When the processions reach the Sungchöra, where the Dalai Lama or Regent and high officials are watching from a balcony, the Nechung Oracle comes out of the south door of the Jokhang in a state of possession and after his ritual dance presents a scarf to the image of Jampa. Scarves are also offered by representatives of the Dalai Lama and officials and the onlookers also add their contribution. The square and street are solid with a crowd of monks and lay people. They are all very orderly, but it is difficult to see what is going on. Eventually way is made for the Dalai Lama's elephant which arrives in elaborate caparison and at a command from the mahout kneels in front of the Dalai Lama's window and trumpets a salute. The Tibetan Government always tried to have an elephant at Lhasa as a symbol of universal sovereignty but there have been intervals when one has died and a

Opposite:
Author at the summit of Gyamberi; ceremonies start when the sunrise strikes it.

replacement has not been found. The Oracle used to be expected to ride on the elephant but that proved too hazardous.

When the procession has passed on towards the entrance of the Jokhang guns are fired from Lubu and from near Kundeling to mark the start of races and sports in honour of the Coming Buddha. A space is cleared in front of the Sungchöra and a mat is laid down on which a succession of wrestlers compete. They are men from the Dalai Lama's bodyguard regiment. They wear small loin cloths and most are rather small and wiry. The bouts are mostly short and spiritless and as soon as there is a fall their seconds hurry to cover them in their cloaks. Only one brawny well-muscled fellow swaggers about challenging all comers; but no one takes him on. Later I heard that the duty is unpopular and the participants feel shame because it is deemed improper to appear naked or nearly so in front of one's superiors. Alongside the wrestlers other men struggle to carry a heavy stone round a mark. All the contestants eventually get a scarf and some money.

While this is going on, the principal events — a series of races by riderless horses, foot runners and mounted men — have got under way. The horses scurry along, driven on by a few mounted grooms. Only the government and leading noble houses and, surprisingly, the small monastery of Lamo are allowed to enter horses and it is a matter of prestige to win. Somehow the government usually manages to get the first prize, helped it is said, by a good deal of skulduggery from its servants who are posted at strategic points to drive rivals off the course.

At the same time a foot race starts from a point nearer the city. The runners are a motley collection of old and young men and boys performing a task imposed on them by their landlords. Before long the first riderless horses gallop into the Barkor and up to the finishing post where they are recorded by official judges. Soon the first runners appear; they wear brightly coloured shirts and drawers and multi-coloured caps. The Capuchin missionary Cassiano Beligatti da Macerata records that formerly they used to run naked but that Pholha Miwang ordered them to wear drawers. The race was perhaps the survival of the practice of ritual nudity for bringing rain known in other eastern civilizations. Only a few of the runners seem interested in winning; most jog along easily, capering and waving to the crowd. Soon there is a confused stream of runners and riderless horses in a confined space and finally the arrival of the mounted men adds to the danger to the runners. They are retainers of the noble houses whose race has started, after the others, from the Bamari overlooking Kundeling quite close to the city. It is surprising that accidents are rare and all the competitors find their way to different finishing points at the south-east corner of the Barkor.

When all the stragglers have arrived the officers in charge of the ceremony mount a platform in the Shar Kyareng, at the south-east end of the Barkor, and distribute prizes and scarves for all the competitors.

Foot runners and horses in the races during "The Invitation to Maitreya".

Everything was over quite early in the day and as we left a room overlooking the Sungchöra and passed above the Khyamra prayer hall on our way out through the Jokhang we saw the Ganden Tri Rinpoché preaching his last sermon to the comparatively small congregation of monks who had remained at Lhasa during the whole three weeks of the Mönlam. After that the monks set off for their monasteries with their books and other possessions in bamboo carrying-frames on their backs. The Ganden Tri Rinpoché and the Shengo returned in state respectively to Ganden and Drepung, and so the Mönlam Chenmo ended. But two further days of lay celebrations remained before the end of the month.

26th Day: The Gallop behind the Fort

རྫོང་རྒྱབ་ཞབས་འབེལ།

The name of this ceremony, the Dzonggyap Shambé, is uncertain. The common version of the spelling is *rDzong-rgyab Zhabs-'bel*, "The Gallop Behind the Fort"; but there is another, *rDzong-rgyab gZhar-'phen*, apparently meaning "The Shooting in Succession Behind the Fort". At all events what happens is a competition between men of the Yaso's cavalry in a display of marksmanship at targets suspended beside a long narrow runway in a meadow north of the Potala and south of the Lhalu mansion.

Tents are pitched there for the Kashag and high officials and for foreign guests; lesser officials sit on rugs on the ground in order of precedence; places are allotted to boys of the Tse school, servants of government offices and the Dalai Lama's dancing boys; and a tent is set up for the cooks who provide the refreshments, in recognition perhaps that this has been an unusually busy month for them.

After the arrival of the Kashag there are the usual formalities. The Yaso present scarves to the Kashag and submit lists of the competitors; and, of course, tea is served. Each squadron provided by the noble houses then takes part separately. One

Target-shooting at "The Gallop behind the Fort", in front of the Lhalu mansion.

Competitors in "The Gallop behind the Fort" salute the Tibetan Cabinet.

after another the horsemen ride down the runway firing with a matchlock with antelope-horn prongs at the first target, then rapidly swinging the gun round their backs they grab the bow and take an arrow from their quiver ready for the next target. Some do not have time to draw the bow but simply thrust the arrow at the target.

When all the men of the right wing have finished the course there is a pause. The Dalai Lama's dancing boys collect the arrows and bring a list of hits to the Labrang Chandzö — the Treasurers of the Jokhang. The competitors then come up by squadrons and receive scarves of different quality according to their score. Then they perform a special Mongolian salute, raising their right hand, then bending the right knee and touching the ground with their hand. They return to their horses which have been left at some distance, with cries of *Lhagyallo*, "Victory to the gods!".

The Kashag then go to lunch and after that the squadrons of the left wing complete their course, receive their scarves and salute. The two Yaso and their retinue come to make a deep bow to the Kashag who then leave in procession. The Yaso go to lead their cavalry in a last circuit of the city on the way back to their headquarters at Lubu from where they are soon dismissed.

That ends the formal ceremonies of the New Year. On the same day, in a remote part of the plain, further to the north, young lay officials who have recently been given a post or who have received promotion hold their own competition, the Trungkhor Tsegyu, in shooting arrows from horseback at targets like those of the Dzonggyap Shambé, away from public gaze. All that remains is a day of relaxation for officialdom to recover from the prolonged duties of the month.

27th Day: Sky Archery

གནམ་མདའ།

The Namda was an occasion of easy conviviality spent at the government summerhouse south of the Lhalu mansion near the site of the Dzonggyap Shambé. Foreign guests are not invited and it is difficult to follow the course of events from written and oral accounts. But it starts with some formality when all lay officials gather to take their seats on the verandah of the summerhouse in usual order of precedence. Tea and rice are served; and the Yaso lead a party of the Zimchongpa, with their standards and another of the horsemen who took part in the Dzonggyap Shambé. They are all served with tea and rice and are given scarves and rewards for the services. The Yaso go to supervise the placing of targets for the archery competitions then come to report to the Kashag that all is ready for the contest. It is then announced formally and loudly by a junior official that there will be contests in shooting long distance and at targets at different ranges. Competitors are chosen to represent the Shappés and other high officials and the shooting begins. Marking is done by the Dalai Lama's dancing boys. During the competition there are several servings of tea and rice. When the archery is finished the marks are reported to the Lachag who submit them to the Kashag. Scarves and prizes are distributed after which the Kashag and high officials retire into the summerhouse for a prolonged banquet of delicacies accompanied by the drinking of *chang* served by maids of honour. Other officials are entertained on the verandah.

After the Kashag return, the day is devoted to light-hearted merriment. Many officials and occasionally some Shappés take their turn to shoot whistling arrows at a target. Whoever scores a hit offers a bowl of *chang* to the Kashag and is offered one by them and the successful archer receives a scarf so that anyone who is a particularly good shot is wreathed in scarves after a time, and a good deal of *chang* is drunk. When that sport is finished there is more tea and food and the company settle down to listen to different traditional songs. The Dalai Lama's dancing boys sing to the accompaniment of flutes and Chinese and Tibetan stringed instruments; the Yaso and their retinue, the Damgya Shokpa (descendants of Gushri Khan's Mongols) and finally the Zimchongpa make their contribution. The party ends well into the evening with farewell scarves and a distribution of eatables to all according to their rank from Shappés to Zimchongpa. After which all stand and salute towards the Potala. The Shappés are escorted to their homes by the Dalai Lama's dancing boys playing the drum-beat appropriate to their rank; and so, presumably, to bed.

The number of scarves presented and bowls of tea drunk during this month must have run into many thousands, all accounted for by one or other of the government offices. All official business was virtually suspended though I did succeed each year that I was at Lhasa in having one meeting with the Foreign Office at the Tsuklakhang.

"Sky Archery".

The Second Month

19th Day: The Great Assembly of Worship

ཚོགས་མཆོད་ཆེན་མོ།

After the eventful days that fill the first month there is an interval before the next great ceremony, the Tsokchö Chenmo. It was instituted according to tradition by the great Regent, Sangye Gyatso (1653-1703), to commemorate the death of the Fifth Dalai Lama in 1682, and that is also stated by Thupten Sangay in his account of the festivals of Tibet. The assembly, which appears to have been a political device for the benefit of the Gelukpa church, to enhance the prestige of the Dalai Lama and consolidate the position he acquired in 1642 as head of Church and State, follows the model of the Mönlam Chenmo but on a smaller scale. The prayer services in the Tsuklakhang lasted for only twelve days and were attended almost entirely by Geshes and learned lamas so that whether by tradition or because the distribution of alms was much smaller, Lhasa was not crowded by a great number of ordinary monks.

On the morning of the first assembly, the Dalai Lama received the abbots of the great monasteries and other high religious dignitaries in his private rooms in the Potala. Later, the Shengo of Drepung arrived in state and once more assumed control of the city. On this day the assembly was attended by the Shappés, perhaps a hint of the crypto-political origin of the ceremony. The senior Shengo read a proclamation by the Seventh Dalai Lama explaining the purpose of the ceremony and then repeated it at several places round the Barkor. Thereafter there were three prayer sessions each day as at the Mönlam Chenmo. On the twenty-fifth of the month a special service was held in commemoration of the death of the Fifth Dalai Lama; and on a chosen day a feast, similar to the Lama Gatön, the priests' banquet, was given to the lamas.

During the Tsokchö Chenmo the rule of the Shengo was less ostentatious and oppressive. The air of awed tension was absent and the ordinary life of the people seemed unaffected. The business of government was hardly interrupted and I could visit the Foreign Office regularly, except on two great public ceremonies, during the twelve days.

There is some uncertainty about the date when the ceremony was instituted. The Fifth Dalai Lama died on the the twenty-fifth of the second month in 1682 but his death was not disclosed until 1697. Sangye Gyatso's *Vaidurya Serpo* indicates that the Tsokchö was established in 1694 as a prayer offering for the great tomb of the Dalai Lama. Perhaps it is to be understood that the construction of the tomb was undertaken during the major building work on the Potala, which was finished in 1695, on the pretext that it was being carried out by the Dalai Lama himself in preparation for his eventual demise. The overt connection with his death would therefore have been made after 1697 until when the prayers were held in honour of the supposedly living Dalai Lama. The problem may be examined more fully elsewhere. The proclamation by the Seventh Dalai Lama about the origins of the Tsokchö Chenmo suggests that there was an interruption following the troubled events after the death of Sangye Gyatso in 1705 and that it was reintroduced after the Seventh Dalai Lama returned to Lhasa in 1735. Shankhawa's account, which implies that the deaths of the Seventh and Eighth Dalai Lamas were also commemorated during the Tsokchö, suggests that the ceremony was subject to later additions. Indeed it is probable that all the ceremonies of the year must have suffered interruptions and changes at various troubled times from the seventeenth century onwards and that their latest form owed much to the Thirteenth Dalai Lama after his return from exile in 1913.

29th Day: The Demon-Ransom King

གླུད་འགོང་རྒྱལ་པོ།

In this ceremony two men dressed in shaggy goatskins and with their faces painted half black and half white are driven out of the city in a performance which has a superficial resemblance to the ritual recorded in other civilizations where a scapegoat is expelled bearing with him the sins of the people. It is usually described in those terms by foreigners who have seen or read about it, but in a wide-ranging article in the *Journal Asiatique* of 1991 Samten Karmay has shown that the Tibetan ceremony is based on a different concept and that the apparent scapegoats called Lügong Gyalpo are a kind of *lü*, a ransom for the *cha*, the good fortune and general wellbeing of an individual. He cites two instances in which the rite was performed for the health of the Regent Sangye Gyatso. It is there called Gyalpo Tsedö. I take this to mean something like "The Best Kingly Sky-Offering". The *dö* here is a type of *torma* consisting of an elaborate contraption of sticks and threads representing the sky; and *tse* perhaps similar to its use in *tsepü*, the best offerings; the king is here identified by Samten Karmay with the deity Pehar. On the first occasion in 1680 the rite lasted for nine days, and the expulsion of a *gong* demon (Lügong) is mentioned. The second occasion in which only the Tsedö is mentioned was on the twenty-ninth of the second month in 1682, that is four days after the death of the Fifth Dalai Lama when Sangye Gyatso was virtually ruler of Tibet. The ceremony at Lhasa in recent times was performed for the life and good fortune of the ruler — the Dalai Lama or, in the interim between the death of one Dalai Lama and the discovery of his reincarnation, for the Regent. It was also held to be for the prosperity of the state, which gave it an incidental resemblance to scapegoat rites held elsewhere. Perhaps Sangye Gyatso introduced an annual performance on that same day — the twenty-ninth of the second month — for his own benefit at first and later for that of the Dalai Lama when the new reincarnation was discovered in 1685 but kept secret until 1697.

It may be noticed that Shankhawa attributes the ceremony to a secret vision of the Fifth Dalai Lama, but that is perhaps a confusion with the Sertreng, the procession on the following day which is traditionally held to have been inspired by such a vision or dream.

The earliest foreign visitor to have described the ceremony was the Capuchin Father Cassiano Beligatti da Macerata who has left valuable information about what he saw in 1742. The beneficiary was then the "King", that is Pholha Miwang who was the effective ruler of Tibet at that time. Several Chinese officials in Tibet during the Manchu period gave what appear to be rather sketchy accounts of it (see Yoshiro Imaeda's article in the *Journal Asiatique*, 1978). Pandit Nain Singh of the Survey of India who was at Lhasa in 1866 mentions it briefly but Gonbojab Tsybikov, a Russian Buriat who was there in 1900, gives a detailed account in his little-known diary, which has recently become available in a French translation. Madame Alexandra David-Neel, famous for her adventurous journey from East Tibet, made her way to Lhasa in 1924 and has written a characteristically lively and perceptive story of what she saw and understood of the ceremony; and T.L. Shen and S.C. Liu give a brief but useful description of it, which they saw sometime in the 1940s. In all the early accounts including that of Madame David-Neel there is mention of only one Lügong. The second is said to have been added by the Thirteenth Dalai Lama who claimed to have discovered after reading the works of the Fifth Dalai Lama that there had originally been two, one from Lhoka and one from Phenpo. He therefore restored the former practice. Perhaps that is what Shankhawa had in mind in his reference to the Fifth Dalai Lama.

In recent times, of the two men on whom the burden fell one was a *poyen*, servant, of the magistrates of the Shö whose other duties were to flog criminals and look after the neighbouring parks; the other was chosen by the villagers of Phenpo who were tenants of the Kundeling monastery in Lhasa. The reported existence of a Lügong

Opposite: *Black Hat dancers before the arrival of the Lügong Gyalpo.*

temple in Phenpo points to an early connection with the rite. Shankhawa says that the Lügong were *gungnyam* of the Dalai Lama, which means literally "of the same age" but may rather be "of the same birth year". I do not know whether any such requirement was actually fulfilled.

In addition to the eyewitness accounts mentioned above René de Nebesky-Wojkowitz in his *Oracles and Demons of Tibet* gives a detailed but not always accurate description of the ceremony derived presumably from information given him by Tibetans in India. The attempt to describe the events from start to finish which follows is based on attendance at the ceremony on three occasions, from information given to me by Tibetan friends, monk and lay, and on the published accounts in Tibetan by Thupten Sangay and Shankhawa Gyurme Sonam Tobgye.

For a week before the twenty-ninth of the month the two Lügong, wearing ordinary clothes but with the small round yellow hat, the *bokto*, worn by junior officials, go round the city carrying black yak-tails and exacting money and presents from shopkeepers, householders and passers-by under the threat of bringing ill-luck on them by a wave of the yak-tail if they do not give. They are said to accumulate considerable sums of money.

Shen and Liu provide the information, not recorded elsewhere, that during this week the monks of the Tantric Gyü college hold services at which a special magic brew of wine is prepared into which each of them spits to ensure its greater potency; and that this is administered to the Lügong on some unspecified occasion.

On the morning of the twenty-ninth the two Lügong have to attend a service at the chapel of Penden Lhamo in a turret on the roof of the Jokhang conducted by the monks of the Nyingmapa monastery of Changchubling, the principal officiants for the whole of the ceremony, who instruct them in the nature of their task and make a dough image as the *lü* of the Dalai Lama — a substitute for his life and prosperity.

Unlike the majority of ceremonies at Lhasa this one does not start until after midday. By then a crowd has gathered around the courtyard in front of the main entrance to the Jokhang. Soon the Kashag and high officials appear on a balcony above the front of the Jokhang. Then the two Shengo of Drepung with their deputies, attended by brawny monk police carrying long poles, staves and sticks, march gravely across the courtyard and sit on a bench below the Dalai Lama's window. A long blast from two silver horns on the west side of the courtyard announces the emergence from the Jokhang of the Changchubling monks who perform a short ritual of exorcism to the accompaniment of oboes and cymbals. When that is finished a party of Black Hat (Shanak) monk dancers, also from Changchubling, wearing tall broad-brimmed black hats surmounted by flame-like fretwork and a conical gold ornament, perform the slow pirouettes of their tantric dance, gesturing with wide, flowing sleeves and holding a skull cup in one hand and a *dorje* in the other. While they dance the *lopön*, the senior teacher of Changchubling, enveloped in a red cloak and wearing a yellow mitre, comes to sit on a high cushioned seat facing the Dalai Lama's window. Several accounts say that the abbot of the Namgye Tratsang sits nearby, but neither my notes nor photographs shows this.

Suddenly there is a deafening outburst of whistling and clapping and a clamour of oboes, cymbals and horns as the two Lügong in heavy goatskin robes and with their faces half black and half white bound out of a side door, "The Lügong's Secret Door" to the east of the Jokhang entrance. They caper wildly round the court brandishing black yak-tails with threatening gestures. The leader of the Black Hats challenges them to defy the faith; and the matter is put to the test in a game of dice with the Changchubling Lama. The Lügong dance around him and slap down their dice in front of him with defiant looks. The lama responds quietly and invariably wins because all his dice are sixes while those of the Lügong are all ones. So it is ensured that there is no danger to the well-being of the Dalai Lama and the prosperity of the State. As the Lügong caper dejectedly, sacks of grain, loads of cloth and other presents are brought to them from the government; and the crowd showers them with scarves and packets of money which their attendants scurry round to pick up. Then to another storm of whistling and clapping, the Lügong leave, one to the south, the other to the north, each firmly gripped by a stalwart

The Lügong Gyalpo is driven out through clapping and whistling crowds.

monk. The departure to the south which was the only one I saw (the other towards the Ramoché temple is said to have been similar in most respects) was led by servants of the Lügong, one of whom carried the *lü* — the dough image of the Dalai Lama; with him were minor officials of the Shö and behind them some monk police. Then came the Lügong in the grip of his monk escort and behind them the Lügong's *torma* of brushwood entwined with entrails followed by a ragged little boy dragging a dogskin. The crowd lining the road kept up the whistling and clapping and showering of the Lügong with money. It was said to be a good opportunity for getting rid of counterfeit coin. The giving of these offerings both then and on previous days shows that the people regarded the Lügong as substitutes for themselves as much as for the Dalai Lama. While the Lügong's servants are gathering up the money four

The servants of the Lügong Gyalpo gather up money thrown to him.

figures in towering fierce masks come to pursue the Lügong; they wear brocade capes and black silk skirts with a demonic face in front and they brandish a short curved knife in one hand and a skull in the other. These are the Ging, messengers of fierce deities such as Pehar. After a short distance they return to dance briefly in front of the Jokhang before going back into it.

The Ging dancers drive out the Lügong Gyalpo

Meanwhile a large *torma* has been brought out, followed by a long file of lamas from the two tantric, Gyü, colleges in ceremonial dress and with long-handled drums and cymbals, who enter the courtyard where one of the abbots performs a service of exorcism with the deep-throated chanting of prayers for which the Gyüpa monks are especially renowned. The service ended, one group marches off after the *torma* on the route taken by the south-bound Lügong; the other goes towards the Ramoché where another *torma* has been prepared. Behind the lamas of Gyü comes the City Magistrate in his official dress of a scarlet cloak with blue facings over a

The torma.

yellow silk robe and with the little yellow *bokto* hat; with him is a servant in brown silk and a wide red "Mongolian" hat. They precede a small group of which the central figures are a youth in yellow silk and a yellow *bokto* hat and a girl in brocade dress with a large white scarf over her shoulders and a curious ornament on her head like a beehive of seed pearls. They carry wands. They are the Pawo and Pamo, who embody the luck of the city. They are supported on either side by a man in silk with a "Mongolian" red hat, carrying a wand, and on the other side by an old woman in an ordinary cloth *chuba*. Behind come two young children. They follow the Lügong to ensure that he does not take away the good luck with the bad; and they return later bringing the good luck with them. After an interval the Ganden Tri Rinpoché, shaded by a yellow state umbrella and preceded by a line of learned lamas, comes from the Jokhang to join the procession. Then in a long, straggly line the motley retinue of the Nechung Oracle files out; and finally to the shrilling of oboes the Oracle himself appears and after dancing briefly is hurried along by two strong monks after the Lügong. When he reaches the open space where the *torma* is waiting he shoots an arrow at it and it is set on fire. He shoots other arrows in all directions before collapsing and being carried back in his travelling chair. The Lügong is then escorted by his attendants and the monk police to the ferry across the Kyichu at

The Nechung Oracle follows the torma.

Ramagang. On the other side he takes off his shaggy cloak. He is given a horse and proceeds on his way to Samye. Thupten Sangay states that another Torgya is performed at Gongkar monastery on the south bank of the Tsangpo, presumably while the Lügong is in that neighbourhood. At Samye he goes to the Ukhang, in the Pehar temple, to the north-east of the main Tsuklakhang, in which the breath of the dead is said to be stored. The locked room is opened and he goes in to deposit the *lü* of the Dalai Lama alongside others there. In the past he had to spend a week in this grim and terrifying room full of fierce masks and other horrors. It is said that some died in terror; but recently, after a short visit to the Ukhang, he is only expected to stay within the precincts for about three weeks. From Samye he is said to go to Tsethang for a few days when he collects other presents before returning to Lhasa. In the past a house was assigned to him on the south side of the Kyichu but that practice has long been abandoned.

The Lügong from Phenpo goes directly back to his village where, presumably, he reports at the Lügong temple before resuming his ordinary tasks.

A torma about to be burnt.

Similar ceremonies take place elsewhere. At Gyantse the counterpart of the Lügong Gyalpo is a strange figure, half-naked with sheep's intestines around his neck, a sheep's stomach over his head like a mask, and an exaggerated phallus below his waist. He is called the Pawo Rolü, the hero corpse ransom.

The Lügong of Gyantse, called the Pawo Rolü.

Overleaf: *The Dalai Lama's dancing boys at the "Golden Procession".*

30th Day: The Golden Procession of the Assembly of Worship

ཚོགས་མཆོད་སེར་སྦྲེང་།

Driving out the Lügong with their burden of ill fortune cleared the air for a peaceful and spectacular ceremony, the Sertreng, in which hundreds of participants marched round the Potala with banners, religious objects and music. The word *sbreng-ba* is used of things happening or joined together in sequence as in the flow of a river or the beads of a rosary (*phreng-ba*), and although *Ser-sbreng* (Sertreng) should strictly be understood as "Golden Procession", it may also be seen, as many Tibetans saw it, as a golden rosary surrounding the Potala.

Once again the Fifth Dalai Lama was the inspiration, for it was instituted by his great Regent Sangye Gyatso in commemoration of a vision seen by the Dalai Lama; but it is not clear whether it was established in his lifetime.

Preparation for the event goes on for several days. The permission of the Dalai Lama has to be obtained to open the treasury of sacred objects — the Chödzekhang — in the north-west corner of the first floor of the Jokhang. A great scroll made for Sangye Gyatso describing the reason for the ceremony and depicting at length and in detail the objects to be carried and the dances and so forth to be performed, is spread round four pillars in an upper room of the Jokhang and is consulted with great care and reverence. The sacred objects are taken out in the presence of representatives of the Dalai Lama, the Kashag and the Treasurers and are arranged in their proper sequence round the inner ambulatory passage of the Jokhang where they are guarded overnight.

Early in the morning of the 30th monks chosen by their teachers from several colleges of the great monasteries assemble at the Jokhang, having washed themselves well and wearing their best robes, yellow hats and brocade *chablu*, water-bottle covers. Each is entrusted with a banner or one of the sacred objects which are a remarkable collection of ancient treasures including images, small paintings, portable shrines, books, mandalas, polished mirrors said to repel dust, incense burners, holy water ewers and bowls, silver-mounted conch shells, musical instruments and many more.

When the sun lights up the summit of Gyamberi, the mountain overlooking Drepung — the usual time signal for most ceremonial events — the procession sets out round the Barkor. It is headed by the master of ceremonies with a stick of incense, followed by a number of learned teachers in robes of fine wool, brocade waistcoats and yellow hats, each preceded by a bare-headed monk carrying a large

Opposite: *Masked dancers at the "Golden Procession".*

yellow, red and blue, fringed, umbrella. Then comes a line of monks in yellow hats each carrying a similar umbrella — there are about twenty or more of them; then a similar number with tall cylindrical banners of bright brocade; then many parties of dancers in all sorts of different dress and masks, and musicians playing long trumpets manned by two monks, cymbals, oboes, horns, and drums of all shapes and sizes. From the Barkor the procession winds its way south to the Lingkor, the outer circuit of the city, and halts at the Lubu meadow where it is reviewed by the officials to see that all is in order before it proceeds at a measured pace across the Turquoise Bridge towards the Potala.

The "Golden Procession": the great Köku banner, with the Shö pillar in the foreground.

The rocky slopes of the Potala hill are already crowded with onlookers who also surround the open space at the west end of the Shö precinct under which lie the state granaries. This is the arena for the following events.

As soon as the leaders of the procession reach the stone pillar opposite the main entrance to the Shö the boom of long horns from the roof of the Potala gives the signal for hauling up the Köku—"The Silk Image"—a great appliqué banner which covers the lower face of the Potala for a space of some 75 by 40 feet. It consists of two panels, one rather larger than the other; in the centre of each is a huge figure of the Buddha surrounded by many deities and bodhisattvas. The privilege of hauling it up is enjoyed by the monks of the Pempora college of Drepung. The bearers of umbrellas, banners and the sacred objects come in and cluster round the edges of the arena. The Shengo of Drepung and many officials in bright ceremonial dress who have gathered in the open space do reverence to the Köku, as do all onlookers. The Kashag arrive and take their place in one of the brilliantly decorated tents arranged on the south side of the arena. They also do reverence to the Köku, and then a prayer service is held in their presence after which they settle down to tea and rice and to watch the ceremony.

First, the Dalai Lama's dancing boys perform to the music of horns and drums, posturing stiffly with occasional sudden leaps as they twirl their ceremonial battle-axes. After them comes a party of stalwart monks with mitre-like hats and wearing blue brocade waistcoats and yellow aprons over their skirts which are hitched up to their knees. They carry large drums on their backs with long ribbons streaming round them as they swirl and leap with great vigour, beating the drums behind their backs with two curved drumsticks. They are monks of the Sakya college of Gongkarchödé south of the Tsangpo near the confluence of the Kyichu. They have had to train for a long time and they alone of the performers are given tea, rice and meat after their dance as a reward for their strenuous performance. Then the long retinue of the Nechung Oracle files in; and the Oracle himself comes from a room in the Shö where he has entered his trance and dances in front of the Kashag brandishing his sword and bow. When he pauses, white scarves are heaped upon him by the Kashag and anyone else who can get near. Then at intervals throughout the morning different dancers in a great variety of dress come in succession. There is a group of small boys in white and blue with elfin masks; figures in golden robes and the headdress of bodhisattvas wearing benignly smiling yellow masks dance with stately movements; others in blue brocade, with crown-like headdresses, flat golden masks, and bone aprons, gesture with *dorje* and bell; others in rainbow-coloured robes beat round drums in front of them. There is an ever-changing pattern of colour and movement: bright umbrellas blowing in the breeze, the rich dresses of the dancers and of officials in their ceremonial robes.

In one interval four tall monks with yellow cloaks and yellow hats march very slowly into the centre and perform with almost imperceptible movements a long formal prostration towards the Potala where the Dalai Lama may be watching. They slowly raise their hands high above their heads and remove their hats, then unfold

Opposite: *Images of the Kings of the Four Quarters join the procession.*

Monks perform a slow-motion prostration to the Dalai Lama, who watches from the Potala.

Below: *Officials surround the Nechung Oracle: four monks in foreground.*

Carriers of banners leave for the procession around the Potala.

their cloaks and very gradually sink to their knees and prostrate themselves with their arms stretched out in front then, as slowly, get up to repeat the interminable prostration twice more before at last putting on their hats and cloaks and marching off. It is said to be an ancient Indian tradition from the great Buddhist monastery of Nalanda. During this long performance other dances go on; and all the time a joker, holding a whip and bucket and leading a cow, prances round the arena teasing the people in reach. The cow is the Döjowé Ba which produces wish-fulfilling milk. He pretends to milk it into the bucket from which he scatters liquid over the crowd. The whole occasion is one of kindliness and good humour, colour and music.

Towards early afternoon the procession gradually moves out of the Shö and on to the road round the Potala. Four elephants of painted canvas are carried out of the Shö followed by four towering papier mâché figures of the Guardians of the Quarters borne on the shoulders of monks. The Dalai Lama's live elephant arrives with beautiful silk and brocade trappings. It kneels and salutes the presence of the Dalai Lama and marches off followed by a fine horse with gilded caparison carrying a gold

Wheel of the Dharma on its back — both are symbols of universal sovereignty. Finally the Zimchongpa in mail armour, many carrying flags on lances, bring up the rear.

The procession moves through the western stupa-gate — the Bargo Kani — and round to the Lukhang park on the north side of the Potala where the performers are allowed to rest and are given tea and rice. The Nechung Oracle, now in monk's dress, rides on to his monastery of Meru preceded by his robes and great helmet on the back of another horse. The people salute it reverently as it passes, for the robes and above all the helmet are more awesome than the wearer. After a long rest the procession moves on by way of the Ramoché temple, where the drum-dancers of Gongkar have to perform again, and back to the Jokhang from where it disperses. The bearers of sacred objects have some time to wait while everything is handed back and accounted for by the Treasurers of the Chödzekhang, so ending a particularly brilliant and enjoyable festival.

The concept was not entirely new. Karmapa records mention of a Sertreng and the displaying of a Köku in the fifteenth century.

The "Golden Procession" seen from the Chakpori.

The Third Month

There are no public ceremonies in the Third Month but on the eighth day, at an occasion called the Gyetor, the officials assemble in the great hall of the Potala for the formal changing from winter into summer dress. The flat, round *soksha* with a fur brim gives way to a light affair with a shady brocade brim and a high crown of red silk tassels with a turquoise ornament on top; heavy fur-trimmed brocades are replaced by robes of lighter material. Newly appointed officials put on the dress of their new post. Nothing significant occurs in Tibet without some religious ritual and on the morning of this day according, to a precedent from the time of the first Dalai Lama, sacred paintings and precious objects are displayed in the hall. Prayers and services are offered to Mahakala.

The first fifteen days of the month are devoted in most monasteries to services of the Kalachakra for which preparation such as the making of mandalas of coloured sand have gone on for several days. On the fourteenth day, according to Shankhawa, the monks of the Namgye Tratsang perform mystic dances for several hours in the great hall of the Potala which are attended by the Dalai Lama, all monk officials and the Prime Minister and Kashag. On the fifteenth the Kalachakra ritual is performed in the great hall in the presence of the Dalai Lama and monk officials.

The Fourth Month

3rd Day: The Great Procession

ཆིབས་བསྒྱུར་ཆེན་མོ།

According to protocol this ceremony, the Chipgyu Chenmo, takes place in the first week of the fourth month but in practice it may be on any day before then, chosen as auspicious for the Dalai Lama to go in procession from the Potala to his summer palace in the Norbulingka. Early in the morning the Kashag, the abbots of the great monasteries, incarnate lamas, and the whole official body, monk and lay, assemble at the Potala.

The short stretch of road from the foot of the Potala hill to the Norbulingka is crowded with onlookers including many monks. The road has been carefully swept and lined with whitened stones; auspicious designs in white, yellow and red chalk have been drawn on the cobbled area in front of the Norbulingka gate; clouds of incense rise from large white pots at intervals along the roadside.

The procession sets out from the north door of the Potala headed by a rider in Mongol dress with a high-peaked hat holding the Sipaho — a *thangka* of cosmic symbols — followed by other horsemen similarly dressed carrying paintings of the Eight Lucky Signs in large round frames on poles; then more, with cylindrical banners on lances. Next comes a long convoy of mules and ponies with various loads under yellow silk covers, containing household goods of all sorts, carpets, furniture and kitchen equipment, accompanied by the Dalai Lama's cooks on horseback wearing monk's dress and tall hats like chef's but of yellow wool; then many brass-bound red leather boxes of robes, religious vessels and other valuables; some of the animals are led by grooms, and senior servants ride at intervals to keep an eye on things. After this seemingly endless line come the Dalai Lama's dancing boys in bright brocade, mounted, playing shrill horns and beating the appropriate rhythm on drums which they hold out in front of them. Then in ascending order of rank ride all but the greatest of the official body, monk and lay, in their new summer dress.

At length comes the Dalai Lama in his golden palanquin carried by twelve bearers in green uniforms and large red hats, and four more in yellow silk. It is preceded by his tutors on horseback and the officer in charge of the palanquin with a number of reserve bearers and several officials in the *gyaluché* dress on foot. The palanquin is shaded by two yellow state umbrellas and one of peacock feathers. On either side ride the Commander-in-Chief and the Commander of the bodyguard regiment in yellow military uniform, and the principal officers of his household in white "boater" hats; and close to it come the regent (in the minority of the Dalai Lama), the Prime Minister, the Dalai Lama's family and members of the Kashag. Behind in single file ride the abbots and incarnate lamas in voluminous scarlet cloaks with three circular white symbols on the back. They are followed by the Dalai Lama's tall monk guards in gilded hats tied under their chins with red ribbons. After them come parties of dancers and singers and the Pawo and Pamo — the boy and girl who embody the good luck of the city, whom I saw walking in the Lügong ceremony.

Finally the procession is brought up by the Dalai Lama's bodyguard regiment preceded by its band and marching with fixed bayonets and colours flying, to loud martial music.

When he arrives in the Norbulingka the Dalai Lama enters his palace of the Kesang Phodrang where he holds a short reception for the usual number of officials. Meanwhile the dancers and singers perform outside the palace. That ends another display of colour and good organization. The troops march back to barracks and the officials wend their way home.There were so many participants in the ceremony that the foregoing account doubtless omits many and misplaces others.

The Chipgyu Chenmo, the "Great Procession" of the Dalai Lama to the Norbulingka.

The Dalai Lama's palanquin in the "Great Procession".

15th Day: Full Moon of the *Saga* Constellation

ས་ག་ཟླ་བ།

The fifteenth of the month (Saga Dawa) when the moon is in the constellation of *Saga* commemorates the Enlightenment of the Lord Buddha and also his death and attainment of nirvana. It is perhaps the holiest day in the Buddhist calendar and the fortnight preceding it is devoted to prayer and religious observances such as fasting. More people than usual make the circuit of the city and special sermons are preached in the Jokhang which many officials attend.

On the fifteenth, from early morning the air is filled with clouds of incense smoke from the leaves of artemisia, scrub rhododendron and juniper twigs in burners on every rooftop and also on surrounding hills. From dawn onwards the whole population sets out to offer scarves and butter for lamps at all the holy places of Lhasa and to walk round the Lingkor, the outer circuit of the city, telling their rosaries and turning their prayer wheels; some prostrate themselves the whole way. The Shappés begin their day at the Jokhang from where they go to Meru, the Ramoché and other temples such as the Jebum Lhakhang, pausing on the way at the office of the City Magistrates to order the release of some prisoners in honour of the day. Then they proceed on the five-mile walk around the Lingkor distributing alms as they go — as do all the other walkers — to the crowd of beggars from Lhasa and outlying villages who have gathered for the occasion. All offices of the Tibetan government also distribute money and food

Pilgrims on the lingkor during the Saga Dawa.

At that time of year — late May or early June — the weather is usually very warm and as most high officials are unused to walking very far the circuit in the full dress of their rank is hard going, even though some may be shaded by an umbrella carried behind them by a servant. Many of our friends used to drop in to the British Mission at Dekyilingka, just off the west side of the Lingkor, for tea and a rest before going on to Norbulingka to offer scarves at the altars and to attend a brief reception by the Dalai Lama.

After that they are allowed to ride to the Potala for a round of visits to the many chapels. From there they walk down to the Lukhang, a small temple of the *naga* deities in a little lake to the north of the Potala. They are rowed out to the temple in leather coracles to make their offerings, after which they repair to a tent among trees on a pleasant green bank by the lake for a rest and a prolonged lunch during which the Lugarpa, a party of dancers, dance and sing for them. They then embark again in the coracles and, shaded by large red laquered umbrellas, make the circuit of the temple. The Lugarpa accompany them in other boats, singing and playing a variety of instruments and making the proper "white" offerings to the *naga* deities. When the Shappés have left, other officials are also rowed round the temple and after them large numbers of the general public who have been enjoying picnics by the lake, dressed in their best clothes, take to the boats and go round the temple with much singing and laughter. It is a joyous and colourful scene. The Shappés pay a final visit to the Ramoché before riding home.

15th Day: The Flower Offering at Gungthang

གུང་ཐང་མེ་ཏོག་མཆོད་པ།

Also on the fifteenth of the month, as I was told, a curious ceremony, the Meto Chöpa, takes place at Tshe Gungthang some fifteen miles east of Lhasa. The great protectress there is a fierce form of Penden Lhamo known as Dralha Chenmo Dökham Wangchukma, "Great Warrior Deity, the Mighty Mother of the World of Sensual Pleasure", whose image with its face veiled is kept in a large *gönkhang*. Her consort is Trip Dzongtsen, the protector deity of Tsecholing monastery, south of the Kyichu, opposite Lhasa. Because of the savage nature of the goddess the two are allowed to meet only on this one day in the year. The image of Trip Dzongtsen, which is shown in photographs from Bell's collection as mounted on a horse, is brought from Tsecholing on the previous day and placed in one of the lesser temples at Gungthang. Also on the fourteenth of the month the Nechung Oracle accompanied by the Shengo of Drepung comes to stay in the Yangön temple at Gungthang where he has his special shrine. Many people from Lhasa come too to spend the night in tents near the monastery.

On the morning of the fifteenth the monks of Gungthang perform a *cham* — a ritual dance — ending with the symbolic sacrifice of a *lingga* image after which a Köku — a great banner with figures of the Buddha and Bodhisattvas in appliqué work — is hoisted on a tall wooden frame in front of the Gungthang temple. The image of Penden Lhamo is brought in procesion from her *gönkhang* and that of Trip Dzongtsen is also brought and the two are set up opposite one another in the front of the Köku. The Nechung Oracle emerges from the Yangön temple possessed by the deity Pehar and after dancing in front of the two images precedes them in procession round the Köku to the usual clamour of oboes, cymbals and horns. Then after a short prayer service the goddess is returned to her *gönkhang* and Trip Dzongtsen is taken back to Tsecholing. The following morning the Nechung Oracle and the Shengo return to Drepung, but many of the people from Lhasa spend the day enjoying picnics among the trees and on the grassy meadow near the great Kumbum Chöten of Tshe.

The image of Trip Dzongtsen at Gungthang during the "Flower Offering".

The great chöten at Tshe Gungthang, 12th-13th centuries.

The Kashag are rowed around the Lukhang, Serpent Temple, on the full moon day of the Saga.

The Dalai Lama aged three shortly after his discovery in Amdo.

The Fifth Month

5th Day: The Birthday Festival

འཁྲུངས་སྐར་དུས་ཆེན།

This day, known as the Trungkar Tüchen, is the birthday of the Fourteenth Dalai Lama and also of the Thirteenth. The Potala and Norbulingka palaces and certain temples are decorated with flags of the colour appropriate to the month, in this case green, incense is burnt on the roof tops and offerings are made. Householders put up green willow branches on their roofs and burn incense.

Early in the morning the Dalai Lama's family are received by him in his private rooms after which he goes to one of the pavilions in the small lake in the Norbulingka where his tutors, principal officers of the household and the Shappés offer scarves and presents. The Dalai Lama gives them a *chaksung* or *sungdü*, a strip of silk, red for monks and blue for laymen, in which he has tied a special knot on which he blows. They then go to another pavilion where the customary morning audience and tea service take place, and where officials offer scarves and special prayers are said.

From there the Dalai Lama's family go to the Trunglha Gönkhang, a small temple among trees some two miles east of Lhasa, which is the home of the Dalai Lama's birth-god. They offer scarves and incense in the temple and then settle down in a summerhouse near the temple where for several days they entertain a series of guests. The members of the British Mission were always invited on one day and after offering scarves to the family and at the temple, enjoyed a friendly party in the shady park.

The *la*, the soul-force, of the Dalai Lama together with those of his predecessors from the ninth to the thirteenth, is said to be in that temple; that of the eighth Dalai Lama, who was born in Tsang, is at Kyitseluding, to the west of Lhasa.

8th Day: The Comparison of the Gods at Nechung

གནས་ཆུང་ལྷ་བསྡུར།

The Nechung Lhabdur is not a regular festival of the month but is held in the monkey year of each twelve-year cycle.

Some eight oracle-priests who become possessed by Pehar or one of his associates assemble in the great courtyard in front of the main temple of Nechung. The Nechung Chökyong is the chief of them all and serves as their host: after him the most important are the Gadong and Darpoling oracles; among the others there is at least one oracle-priestess. Many people come out from Lhasa and are allowed into the courtyard and to sit or stand on the balconies surrounding it which are decorated with bright hangings. The visiting oracle-priests sit in tents on the south side while all round it stand the retinues of the Nechung and the other oracles in various dress of armour, brocade robes, magicians' hats and curious masks with their trident-headed banners. First, ritual dances are performed by Black Hat magicians and many others with fierce masks, some in skeleton dress, others in black robes, others in blue and green chequered cloaks. The dances are accompanied by the drone of long

"The Comparison of the Gods" at Nechung.

The Nechung Oracle, Ta Lama Lobzang Namgye.

horns, cymbals and drums. After they have finished, the noise intensifies and is joined by the shrilling of oboes and cornets as the Nechung Oracle comes on to the steps of the temple in a state of possession. All the other oracle-priests crowd into the courtyard and also enter a trance. The onlookers swarm all round the oracles offering scarves and there is so much noise, confusion, waving of brightly coloured banners and so on that it is difficult to see what is going on. One of the oracles called Ponya seems to be something of a comic turn, for the people make fun of him. Eventually the oracles go back to their tents to recover and after a while all but the Nechung walk or rather straggle round the temple surrounded by their attendants and a crowd of admirers.

15th Day: The Universal Incence-Offering

འཛམ་གླིང་སྤྱི་བསང་།

The festival of the Dzamling Chisang commemorates the preparation for the founding of the Samye monastery when Padmasambhava subjugated the gods, *nagas* (serpent spirits) and local deities and made them protectors of the Buddhist faith. The people then offered incense to them.

At Lhasa quantities of incense are burnt on the roofs of every holy place and household and also on the hills round the city. Everyone from the nobles down pitches a tent or canopy in one of the parks to the east and south of the city and prepares to enjoy a day of amusement and picnicking. But first, people go to consult their special oracle, for there are many minor prophets in addition to the State Oracles of Nechung and Gadong and the Sera oracle of Karmashar.

On one occasion I went to see the Darpoling oracle whose temple is in the middle of Lhasa. He became possessed three times, on each by a different form of the god

The Darpoling Oracle at the "Universal Incense Offering".

The sacks containing the breath of the dead are carried into the temple of the Darpoling Oracle.

Pehar. In the first he wore similar robes, ornaments and headdress to those of the Nechung Oracle. He danced down the steep and narrow stone stairs outside his temple and on to the street below. There he finally twisted the blade of his sword into a knot and hurled it among the surrounding crowd. In the second he wore a brocade hat with a small brim and a crown of red silk. Again he danced down the steps throwing knives as he went. In his third appearance he had a headdress like the coiled turban worn by images of the Religious Kings of Tibet, but rising out of a sort of tiara of minature skulls. During this dance too he hurled knives, some of which hit bystanders, fortunately on thick clothes. People do sometimes get wounded and on rare occasions killed. If that happens the oracle-priest is heavily fined. Accompanying him at the foot of the stairs were two half-naked figures carrying on their backs black leather sacks with white eyes painted on them; they are supposed to contain the breath of the dead.

Going from there to a party in one of the parks to the east of the city we came upon the Karmashar, the special oracle of Sera. He was seated on a throne in his robes with an attendant standing beside him. Both were drinking copious draughts of *chang*. He was supposed to be in a trance but as he had been sitting and drinking there for several hours it was plain that he was merely miming, and soon after we arrived he got down from the throne, removed his headress, wiped his brow and staggered off. Going home late in the afternoon we passed through the tents of the merrymakers who were laughing, singing and playing musical instruments. It was typical of Tibetan good nature that there was no hint of quarrelling or bad behaviour.

The Sixth Month

4th Day: The Fourth of the Sixth Month

དྲུག་པ་ཚེས་བཞི།

This celebrates the First Turning of the Great Wheel of the Dharma, the preaching of the Doctrine at Sarnath by the Lord Buddha. It is another day for devotional visits to holy places, with scarves and butter for the lamps and the burning of incense on every roof. Crowds circumambulate the Lingkor and visit the Jokhang, Potala, Ramoché, Chakpori and all other temples of Lhasa, and many go on pilgrimage to hermitages in the hills and valleys to the north and east of the city, such as Phabongkha, Phurbuchog, Ke'utsang and the hermitages on the hills behind Drepung and Sera. After a long day of such visits they relax once more in tents in the parks with music and singing and good things to eat and drink.

This day is also associated with King Songtsen Gampo who is said by tradition to have introduced Buddhism to Tibet in 642 A.D., although the manner of this connection seems fairly inappropriate. A drinking mug, *trungben*, which he is said to have thrown from the roof of the Potala in a drunken frolic and which survived unbroken, is ceremonially taken to the Dalai Lama's morning reception for officials and offered to those present, who ritually flick a drop of its contents into the air. On the following two days it is taken round by its custodians to the houses of the Shappés and other high officials. One year a friend among the custodians brought it to me as a great honour so that I could make the ritual offering. It was a simple earthenware mug in a protective silver cover. It is said that the mug was concealed after the end of the kingdom and recovered by Tsongkhapa in a hillside near Lhasa, where its imprint is still to be seen.

25th Day: The Eighth Dalai Lama's Birthday

རྒྱལ་དབང་བརྒྱད་པའི་འཁྲུངས་སྐར་དུས་ཆེན།

The birthday of the Eighth Dalai Lama (1758-1804) is celebrated at Kyitseluding where the Gyankara, a company of the Ache Lhamo dancers who have come to Lhasa in preparation for the Shotön festival in the following month, perform in honour of the god Lichinhara, the Trunglha, birth-god, of the Eighth Dalai Lama.

Ache Lhamo dancers.

29th Day: The Start of the Curd Feast

ཞོ་སྟོན་འགོ་བཙུགས།

This sees the first stages of the Shotön, the Curd Feast, during which companies of dancers perform the musical dramas popularly known as Ache Lhamo. There are several opinions about the reason for the name. One story links it with Pandit Atisha (982-1054), but it may more probably be so called because the monks enjoyed refreshing curds at the end of their Yarné, when they were immured in their monasteries for a hundred days at the height of summer to read through the religious canon. In other parts of Tibet the dances are part of the harvest festival, and curds would be served at the feast which followed.

At all events although curds are regularly eaten during the festival at Lhasa, that is incidental to the primary activity which is the performance of dramas having a religious or moral lesson mostly derived from Indian Buddhist legend or *jataka* stories known as *namthar*, which implies progress towards deliverance. There is a special favourite with the people of Lhasa which recounts how the ingenious minister Gar won a Chinese princess as a bride for his master the King Songtsen Gampo and how she brought the image of the Jowo Rinpoché to Lhasa, thus introducing Buddhism into Tibet.

The Ache Lhamo dances are attributed to Thangtong Gyalpo, a saint of the fourteenth and fifteenth centuries famous for building iron chain bridges in many parts of Tibet as well as many hermitages and the great Kumbum stupa at Chung Riwoché, near Lhatse. At all performances, in the centre of the dancing area, is an altar on which stands his image behind which is a willow tree. It is said that his purpose was to pacify a mountain demon who sought to interrupt the monks during their services at the Yarné retreat. The story has somehow become attached to the Drepung monastery and to a demon dwelling in the hillside above the monastery. The willow tree behind the altar symbolizes the worship of the deities of the earth.

The dramas are performed by a number of long-established companies whose duty it is to appear at the Shotön. The oldest is the Pündün from Chongye, followed by the Tashishöpa from Yarlung and the Gyankara from Rimpung, all of which places are the seats of former rulers of Tibet. In addition there are parties from Nyemo, Chung Riwoché — the home of Thangtong Gyalpo — and Kyomolung in Tölung, and others, ten in all. Almost all the companies consist of men only, including ordinary villagers, small traders and even a few monks; but at least one of the newer groups had women members.

The performers wear dress and in some cases masks by which they can be readily identified. The young men who play the heroine are heavily rouged and powdered and wear a flowered headdress; princes and ministers wear hats like those of the Shappés; lesser officials have huge flat yellow woollen hats; the wicked queen who appears in many dramas has a green mask; and there is a host of lesser characters, messengers, servants, hunters, boatmen, fishermen, executioners, Brahmans, also animals such as monkeys, lions, dragons and so on. All have their part in the various trials and adventures of innocent heroes or heroines, which end after a day-long ordeal, in the triumph of virtue.

The play is every day introduced by three figures, one of whom is the eponymous Ache Lhamo, the Sister Goddess, another is a sort of herald or chorus master, and the third is the leader of the Tashishöpa dancers who perform an introductory dance in white masks and the guise of hunters.

The story is outlined in rapid recitative in a high-pitched voice and when the leading actors come to tell in long arias of their trials and sorrows, or their wicked plans, these too are delivered at the top of the voice. These arias are very popular with all Lhasa and can be heard sung by all classes of society at parties or piercingly declaimed by light-hearted travellers. Acting by the leading figures and the expression of feeling are confined to formal stately gestures, but the lesser figures are allowed more freedom and some degree of comedy. Although the quality of the dresses is specially noted by the audience, props are minimal; a chair stands for the top of a mountain or the roof of a house, taking a whip signifies mounting a horse; if a river is to be crossed, the passengers stand in a canvas frame manned by two boatmen. After every exchange of arias or incidental action, one of the characters ends with a loud shout sounding like "Aha la so", and the rest of the company, who have been ranged around the arena, launch into a dance spinning their bodies round with a great swirl of their ample, belted tasselled skirts as they circle the arena to the exciting beat of a drum and clash of cymbals. Those are the only musical accompaniment, and a different drum-beat marks the entry of each character. There are also interludes of light relief in immensely popular comic turns by leaders of the company, some of whom display real talent. In particular one elderly, thin little man with a scraggy beard brilliantly mimed anything from an old village woman picking up yak dung, to a skittish nun, an oracle in a trance, a pompous official and sometimes even a foreign visitor.

On their arrival at Lhasa all the companies have to report to the Tsechak, the Treasurers of the Potala, who are in charge of the ceremony; after which they go to the east courtyard of the Potala, the Deyang Shar, to give a short rehearsal of parts of their repertoire and then on to do the same at Norbulingka and Drepung.

30th Day: The Curd Feast at Drepung and Sera

འབྲས་སྤུངས་དང་སེ་ར་ཞོ་སྟོན།

This is an important occasion at Drepung on which a great Köku banner like that shown on the Potala in the second month — is spread out on a smooth rock-face to the west of the monastery. A prayer service is held in front of it, and then the Shengos and their assistants formally hand over office to their successors, after which there is a feast at which curds are served.

Later in the day Ache Lhamo dances are performed in the courtyards of some of the monastic colleges. The members of the British Mission were always invited to

Opposite:
Drepung Monastery (above), Sera Monastery (below).

the Kongbo Khamtsen, which had the traditional right of looking after visitors from India.

This was a pleasantly informal occasion and the college authorities received us most hospitably and entertained us to tea and lunch. The courtyard where the dances took place was surrounded by parents and relations of the monks who came, often from considerable distances, in their best clothes, as honoured guests. It was delightful to see the affectionate care and charming good manners with which the monks from the smallest up looked after their guests, serving them with tea, rice and noodles. There was a cheerful, friendly atmosphere, and the performance was much more relaxed than the strictly formal ceremony it was to become at Lhasa. The players frequently broke off for a drink of tea or *chang* at the side of the courtyard and the audience clearly enjoyed it all including such incidents as when a small boy was seen in the swirling dance to have omitted to put on his pants and was sent off to dress properly; and, of course, the comic interludes were rapturously received. At the end of the day the performers were rewarded with scarves and presents to which we contributed; and we were politely escorted to the gate of the monastery.

Preparing the Köku banner for the Curd Festival at Drepung.

The Curd Feast was held at Sera on the same day and we sometimes went there before going on to Drepung. The event at Sera was a visit from their special oracle, the Karmashar in the form of the deity Chatri Chenchig, a minister of Pehar. He

The Karmashar Oracle and attendant demons during the Curd Festival at Sera.

wore robes and a tall, heavy, plumed helmet like those of the Nechung Chökyong and was attended by two figures in fierce masks, called Pendra (*Pe-har-'dra?*), who wore a shoddy imitation of the dress and helmet of an oracle. There was also a small retinue in demon masks said to have been recruited from the *ragyapa*, the cutters-up of the bodies of the dead. The Karmashar Oracle was received with great respect by a group of monks and, in a state of possession, uttered his prophecies for the coming year. These were interpreted and recorded by his secretary. A copy was displayed at the monastery and another on the wall of the Karmashar temple at Lhasa, where it was read and often copied by members of the public.

The Seventh Month

1st - 5th Days: The Curd Feast at Lhasa

ཞོ་སྟོན།

On the first of the month an extended rehearsal is held at Norbulingka by the leading Ache Lhamo companies.

From the second day and the four succeeding days the formal ceremony takes place, with a different company performing a different drama on each day.

Before the present Dalai Lama was discovered it was held in the courtyard of the Regent's monastery at Shidé and thereafter in the large paved open space to the east of the Kesang Phodrang in Norbulingka, where it could be watched by the Dalai Lama from a window hung with yellow silk. On a ledge below the window, decorated

The gate of the Norbulingka Palace.

Opposite: *The image of the Jowo Rinpoché being brought by the princess from China as enacted during the drama of the Chinese and Nepalese Princesses.*

with pots of flowers, were places for the Dalai Lama's tall monk bodyguards. The arena was covered by a huge decorated canopy. In the centre stood the altar of Thangtong Gyalpo and the willow tree. On the north side was a long open tent with seats of the height appropriate to their rank for the Prime Minister and the Dalai Lama's father, and at lower level for the Kashag and other high officials; lesser lay officials sat on cushions in front. On the south were tents for incarnate lamas, abbots and high monk dignitaries, while ordinary monks sat in front; there were also tents for the British and Nepalese Missions. The east side was open for the general public who came in large numbers and were joined by the great ladies of Lhasa in all their finery, which was *de rigueur* for the occasion. Behind the crowd the Dalai Lama's bodyguard were stationed with their band. Members of the British Mission were regularly invited for one or two days.

Ache Lhamo drama at the Norbulingka Palace during the Curd Festival.

The performance was strictly monitored by an official of the Tsechak's office who followed it with a book in his hand, and any lapse would be punished by a fine. When lunch time came there was no interruption to the performance, but the officials filed out solemnly to another tent while we were taken to be entertained in the private rooms of one of the Dalai Lama's principal monk attendants, the Drönyer Chenpo or the Zimpön Khenpo. Afterwards we would walk in the Norbulingka garden before settling down until the end of the day, which might not come until late in the evening. Then the band of the Dalai Lama's bodyguard regiment burst out with a strident rendering of God Save the King, which the Tibetans had adopted as a salute to the Dalai Lama. It was not Tibetan custom to stand up while it was played.

Scarves were hung on the altar and willow tree and presents were brought for the performers — sacks of grain, flour, meat and butter as well as packets of money and of course scarves. The principal actors would join in singing their thanks and praise, and lesser characters when they came to receive their share performed a little step dance and recited some comic form of thanks.

The yak-dancers at the Curd Festival.

On the last day of the Shotön, a great heap of incense is built on a paved space close to the east wall of the Kesang Phodrang. The Dalai Lama comes down from his room and sits on a chair with all the highest officials round him. The incense is lit and a great plume of fragrant smoke rises into the sky. The Dalai Lama and his ministers throw a handful of flour into the air and led by the Zimgakpa, the monk bodyguards, all shout *Lhagyallo*.

The people of Lhasa look forward eagerly to the Ache Lhamo, where they renew memories of favourite songs and scenes which often reduce them to tears for the sorrows and trials of the heroes and heroines.

After the formal ceremony the Ache Lhamo dancers were often engaged by the noble families and wealthy merchants to perform in the courtyards of their houses or in their parks. There was some competition to provide the finest ornaments and dresses, which were regarded as almost as important as the plays themselves. Another small party, the Sherong Drongtsepa, the Wild Yak Dancers, who were not part of the Ache Lhamo companies but whose act was considered to be auspicious, were allowed to go round showing their dance of two lively, realistic pantomime yaks.

10th Day: The Tenth Day Festival at Yerpa

ཡེར་པ་ཚེས་བཅུ།

This small festival of Yerpa Tsechu takes place at Tra Yerpa some eighteen miles from Lhasa. Here a lovely quiet valley contains a group of cave hermitages and small temples associated with the names of Songtsen Gampo, Padmasambhava, Pandit Atisha and other holy men. A prayer service is held followed by religious dances to commemorate the founding of a temple there at the same time as the Lhasa Jokhang. It is attended by many people from Lhasa.

The Tra Yerpa hermitage in a secluded valley east of Lhasa.

1st - 15th Days: The Circumambulation of the Fields

ལྷ་ས་འོང་བསྐོར།

This is a harvest festival, known as the Ongkor, which takes place on an auspicious day in the first half of the seventh month. *Ong-ga* appears in Chödrak's dictionary as meaning *zhing-ga*, "field". In the morning a procession is led by a horseman carrying a *thangka* of the *sipé khorlo*, hung about with a white scarf, and a hail-dispelling *ngakpa* priest followed by a smartly dressed girl and boy representing the Pawo and Pamo ("Hero and Heroine"), the luck bearers of the village, carrying arrows in their hands; then come the landowners on horseback dressed in silk *chubas* and round yellow *bokto* hats which they may only wear on festival days; and after them the villagers, men and women, on foot, some of the men dressed in silk and wearing large round red woolly hats (the *soksha*) while the women sport their best jewelry and bright silk blouses; on their backs they carry volumes of the scriptures. They march all round the boundaries of the village fields chanting prayers and singing harvest songs. After the circuit they make for tents pitched on an open space to sit down to a great feast with quantities of meat and drink. This lasts well into the evening after which a pile of incense is burnt to cries of triumph and the throwing of flour into the air. On the following day the village headmen present scarves to the Dalai Lama through his monk body-guard, and on some later day they are admitted to the Dalai Lama's reception where they offer a token sample of the harvest. That happens only in villages in the near neighbourhood of Lhasa. Elsewhere at similar processions a village priest or a *ngakpa* may lead it; and the harvest offering is made to the abbot of the local monastery.

The Eighth Month

The Bathing Festival

གཟིམ་ཆུང་ཆབ་ཞུགས།

Early in the month the end of the monks' Yarné, summer retreat, coincides with the rising of a star known as Richi (or Rishi) Karma — perhaps Sirius — when it is believed that the water of rivers and springs confers special benefit to health. Although for many days after the Shotön people have been bathing and washing their clothes, the appearance of the star is an occasion for the Chapshu, the Bathing Festival, which is a particular devotion to such activities and it is greatly enjoyed by the monks after their months of immurement. It is also the start of a week or ten days of parties given by government offices and privately by monks and laymen in the city and in monasteries and villages throughout the country.

The Ninth Month

22nd Day: The Divine Descent

ལྷ་བབས་དུས་ཆེན།

The twenty-second of the month sees the Lhabap Tüchen which commemorates the legendary descent of the Lord Buddha from Ganden, the Tushita heaven, where he had been to visit his sainted mother; after which he went to Kasi (Benares). It is a day for much burning of incense and for everyone from the Dalai Lama down to visit the chapels of the Jokhang and Potala for prayer and to offer scarves and butter for the lamps; as usual on such occasions the day ends with feasting.

The Tenth Month

The Procession to the Potala

ཆིབས་བསྒྱུར་ཡར་ཕེབས་དང་ཚོགས་ཕེབས།

On an auspicious day the Dalai Lama sets out from the Norbulingka on his way to his winter palace in the Potala. The state procession is similar to that in the other direction, but this time the route goes north of the Potala through the centre of the city. It is met at a point north of the Tsuklakhang by the Nechung Oracle, after which it proceeds southwards by the east and south sides of the Barkor to the entrance to the Tsuklakhang where the Dalai Lama is escorted to his rooms, the Lateng Zimchung, where he will stay for one or two days. In the courtyard outside the main door singers and dancers perform in his honour. On an auspicious day the Dalai Lama holds an elaborate reception in the Ewam hall in the course of which recently appointed officials do homage. After that the Dalai Lama proceeds to his winter quarters in the Potala.

14th - 15th Days: The Mountain Visit of the Glorious Goddess

དཔལ་ལྷའི་རི་བྲ།

For some days before the fourteenth of the month the monks of Meru, who have living quarters and a prayer hall on the third floor of the Tsuklakhang, hold prayer services in honour of Penden Lhamo, the Chief Protector of the Faith, at her chapel on the same floor in preparation for the forthcoming ceremony.

On the fourteenth, before dawn, the image of the deity, which is made of stone and is said to be a *terma*, hidden treasure, discovered in the twelfth century by Lama Shang of Tshe, is regilded and repainted by the *lharipa*, specially trained painters of religious images, with pigments provided by the treasurers of the Potala and

Jokhang; it is also adorned with jewelry and new robes. Then it is taken from the chapel and set up outside on a broad platform on which are a huge bronze incense burner and another, full of prayer flags on sticks (*darchok*). The monks of Meru perform a special Torgya ceremony, which is attended by the Kashag and the whole official body who present scarves to the deity. They are followed by large numbers of the people of Lhasa who offer scarves, incense and butter for the lamps. A group of ladies led by those of noble birth, known as Pesoma, come in all their finery to sing hymns in honour of the goddess. At the end of the service the *darchok* are scattered and it is considered great good fortune to secure one. In the evening the image of the goddess is taken down to the main temple and set up for the night, facing the Jowo Rinpoché.

The following morning the image on a wooden carrying frame is borne through the main door of the Tsuklakhang on the shoulders of a stalwart monk of Meru who has spent the past week in solitary meditation and prayer in preparation for his ordeal. A great crowd of officials, people of Lhasa, Bhutanese and Nepalese is waiting to shower scarves on it. Its black and hideous face with glaring eyes and a savage grin is surmounted by a large gold headdress like that of the Nechung Oracle but with scarlet plumes. On its chest is a huge silver breast-plate. The long silk robes with a mask of Mahakala on the black apron totally envelop the monk who carries the frame supporting the heavy burden. He is guided by another monk at his side as he moves with short quick steps bearing the goddess in procession round the Barkor where many spectators have gathered. The procession is headed by monks of Meru with long-handled drums, cymbals and oboes, and others with silver censers. After them come masked dancers, and the image is immediately preceded by monks and lay officials carrying incense sticks. It is shaded by a peacock-feather umbrella; and more dancers follow.

The procession halts at certain points where a brief Torgya is performed while the dancers dance and the monk carrying the image gets a chance to sit on a chair which is carried behind him, and to be refreshed with tea. Long silver horns have been set up at each halting place, and boom incessantly. At the Ganden Darchen the tall prayer mast at the north-east corner of the Barkor the Karmashar Oracle in a state of possession by the god Chatri Chenchig is waiting to offer a scarf. Further on, at the Shar Kyareng prayer mast at the south-east corner, the Nepalese representative at Lhasa, in full dress under his state umbrella and with his bodyguard in scarlet tunics, offers a scarf and a bag of gold. The procession then makes a detour to the Lubu meadow for another Torgya. While this is taking place Penden Lhamo's husband, the protecting deity of the Tsecholing monastery, Trip Dzongtsen, is brought out of his *gönkhang* and allowed to regard his fierce spouse from a safe distance across the river. The procession returns to the Barkor and after halting in front of several of the noble houses where rich presents are offered, the image finally

arrives safely at the Tsuklakhang where a last Torgya is performed at which a dough image is broken up and thrown to the crowd. The goddess then re-enters the Tsuklakhang to the relief of its brave bearer.

The name of this ceremony, Pelhé Rito, is obscure and there are several variants (*dPal-lha'i Ri-gra, dPal-ldan Ri-khrod*). My suggestion that the second part of the name is a corruption of *rim-'gro*, "worship", was rejected by Tibetan scholars, and it has recently been explained by Shankhawa that the name was originally *dPal-lha'i Ri-rab*, referring apparently to the goddess taking her seat on the holy mountain Rirab — the mythical Mount Sumeru, the centre of the world. It may be significant that the *torma* sacrifices burnt during the circuit of the Barkor were in the form of *dö*, so-called thread crosses, but which were actually cage-like structures of sticks around which were woven cobweb patterns of thread and other materials and which included among other ritual offerings a representation of Rirab, ofen associated with fierce deities.

Opposite: *Penden Lhamo, the "Glorious Goddess".*

24th Day: The Offerings on the Twenty-Fourth Day at Sera

སེ་ར་བཞི་མཆོད།

This ceremony takes place at Sera in commemoration of the death of Jamchen Chöjé Shakya Yeshe who founded the monastery, the full name of which is Sera Thekchenling, in 1419 some time after his return from China where he had spent several years as spiritual instructor to the Ming emperor Yunglo who sought to make contacts with all the leading lamas in Tibet. Tsongkhapa had received an invitation from him to visit the imperial court but expressed his inability to go and sent his disciple Jamchen Chöjé in his place. His visit was presumably some time after that by the famous Karmapa Deshin Shekpa who was there from 1407 to 1409 as teacher of the emperor; his visit was commemorated in a remarkable scroll describing both in writing and in illustrations the miracles which the lama performed on twenty-two successive days. Many people from Lhasa visit the monastery to offer butter or oil for the thousands of little earthenware lamps which the monks arrange in the evening on window ledges, balconies and parapets all round the monastery.

25th Day: The Offerings on the Twenty-Fifth Day at Ganden

དགའ་ལྡན་ལྔ་མཆོད།

This is the commemoration of the death in 1419 of the Je Rinpoché, Tsongkhapa, the founder of the Gelukpa sect, who instituted the Mönlam Chenmo at Lhasa in 1409 and in the same year founded the monastery of Ganden Nampargyelweling, the first of the Gelukpa monasteries. It is the day when officials change into winter dress in which they present themselves at the Dalai Lama's morning audience in the Potala, after which they and the general public go round the tombs of the Dalai Lamas in the Potala to offer scarves and incense. In the evening great numbers of little lamps are lined up all over the façade of the Potala and on the buildings of the Shö at its foot, and also on every monastery, temple and private house in the city. The whole occasion is known as the Ngamchö, "The Offerings on the Twenty-fifth Day". In the evening friends are entertained and people go about admiring the lights which, if the weather is calm, are a lovely sight.

Ganden Monastery.

The Eleventh Month

4th - 5th Days: The Conjunction of Nine Evils

ངན་པ་དགུ་འཛོམས།

This occasion, the Ngenpa Gudzom, is hardly either a ceremony or a festival. It is a reminder of the fate of some legendary unfortunate who committed nine offences in one day. In order to avoid such a disaster it is advisable to refrain from action of any sort that might cause offence, even unwittingly. So no official or private business is conducted. Strangely this is observed for only half of each day on the fourth and fifth of each month. By evening the danger apparently is over and restrictions are lifted to allow parties to be given by the Dalai Lama's household officials in the Potala and by government officers and private persons elsewhere. It is also the duty of the housewife to sweep the house thoroughly on those days.

The Twelfth Month

27th Day: The Sera Phurbu

སེ་ར་ཕུར་བུ།

On the morning of the twenty-seventh the most sacred treasure of Sera, a *phurbu* ritual dagger with the head of Tamdrin (Hayagriva) as its handle, is taken in procession to Lhasa for veneration by the Dalai Lama and ministers. It is supposed to have been discovered by an Indian yogin and to have flown from India to a hill near Phurbuchog in the Sera valley.

29th Day: The Votive Offering of the Twenty-Ninth Day

རྩེ་དགུ་གཏོར།

The year draws to a close with the Tse Gutor, a solemn performance of *cham*, Tantric dances, to purge the accumulated sins and mischances of the past and to clear the way for the year to come. Of the whole cycle of ceremonies, it is the most deeply charged with mystic, almost sacramental, significance. The monks of Namgye Tratsang who take part have undergone training for many years not only in the steps of the dances and their accompanying music but also in the inner meaning of each movement and gesture. From the early hours of the morning they have engaged in prayer and meditation, each envisaging himself as the deity whose robes and mask he will wear and in which he will be vested with ritual seriousness.

The setting for the ceremony is the great eastern courtyard of the Potala, the Deyang Shar. It is entered by a long, steep, triple stair below which is a well-proportioned flight of stone steps. The wide central windows of the façade above are hung with bright valances; the uppermost, curtained with yellow silk, is that of the private room of the Dalai Lama from which he may watch the dances; the two below are for the Kashag and other senior officials respectively. Over the head of the stairway is a fine brocade curtain. On the north side of the courtyard a long canopy, beautifully decorated with designs in blue and with a large demon head in the centre, shelters the padded seats for the monk orchestra. An open parapet above it provides a viewpoint for spectators as does a similar parapet to the south beneath which are galleries for ladies and other distinguished persons. Towering over the east end is a massive three-storied building reached by a long stone stairway from the Shö. At one side is a balcony for lesser officials and the central windows are reserved for foreign visitors.

The day begins soon after dawn with a parade and show of arms by the Zimchongpa similar to that at the Mönlam Torgya in the first month. When they have displayed their skill, at some length, with their different weapons to the accompaniment of shrill trumpeting, battle cries, taunts and chanting, ending with a loud explosion of musketry, they sit in the courtyard to receive their reward of tea and meat, and then withdraw to the sides. A large crowd, mainly monks, gathers round the foot of the stairs, and others find places round the sides of the courtyard or on the surrounding parapets. As befits a religious occasion there is hardly any noise or chattering.

After a pause a small party of monks wearing cloaks and tall yellow hats take up position at the east end of the courtyard, facing the stairway. Three prolonged

left: The Zimchongpa on the roof of the Jokhang.

The Zimchongpa rally on the morning of the "Votive Offering of the Twenty-Ninth", the Gutor.

The "Lay Officials for a Month" with the Zimchongpa at the Gutor.

boomings from long silver horns at the head of the stairs announce the beginning of the religious ceremony. The orchestra of the Namgye Tratsang monks in ceremonial dress file into the courtyard from the entrance to their college to the south side of the stairway, beating long-handled drums, clashing cymbals and playing oboes and thigh-bone trumpets. Four of them carry two long silver horns to be set up in the centre of the orchestra. All turn in respect towards the Dalai Lama before taking their seats under the canopy.

Another booming summons from the horns invites a party of masked figures who slowly descend the stairs unto the courtyard. The chief is the Chinese priest Hashang, a huge heavily padded figure in a scarlet robe and with a massive smiling, bald-headed mask. With him are two tiny child-like figures, two more in the dress of Indian sadhus, and two with death's head masks. They turn and bow to the Dalai Lama before marching slowly across the courtyard to sit or stand at the eastern end for the rest of the day.

Then at another blast from the horns two masked dancers slowly descend the stairs. One of these is the Chögye Shinjé, the Lord of the Dead and Chief Protector of the Buddhist Faith. He wears a massive yak-head mask and fine robes of dark silk with embroidered apron and sleeves. With him is his consort Tsamuntri who has a stag's head mask. To the music of the orchestra and the steady rhythm of the cymbals

The monks of Namgye Tratsang summon the dancers at the Gutor.

played by the leader they pirouette slowly and gravely with deep concentration and perfect balance, stretching out their wide-sleeved arms and one leg as they turn. After a while they dance back up the stairs and into the Potala. They are followed by seven other pairs of dancers in succession, a principal and his or her consort. They are the Gönpo, wrathful protector deities of the faith who are the retinue of Shinjé. Among them are Dorje Jigje with a bull's head, Tamdrin the horse-headed, a red masked Mahakala, and the black-faced Lhamo. Others have the heads of animals — ape, boar, vulture, garuda, and lastly a white lion and the sea monster, *makara*. They, too, pirouette solemnly but each pair to a subtly different rhythm marked out by the cymbals of the leader of the orchestra.

When the last pair have gone back to the Potala there is a quickening of the tempo of the orchestra and to a burst of whistling and piercing oboe notes, four skeleton figures, graveyard ghouls, messengers of Shinjé, scamper down into the

Black Hat dancers headed by the Dorje Lopon.

Masked dancer descends steps into the courtyard.

court. They wear close-fitting scarlet tights, outlined with the bones of a skeleton, death's head masks and bone aprons. They dance swiftly and vigorously, gesticulating with long bony fingers around the effigy of a human corpse which they have laid on the ground. As they are leaving, an old man with a long white beard and carrying a stick totters in and after a few unsteady steps, collapses on the ground. Servants come to offer him a bowl of fruits but before he can take any, some of the spectators rush in and seize them. A tiger skin is brought and laid on the ground. The old man grapples with it, beating it with his stick and rolling over and over. Eventually he leaps up, wraps it around him and performs a lively dance before marching in triumph back to the Potala. This strange interlude was introduced by the Thirteenth Dalai Lama as the result of a performance he had seen during his exile in Mongolia and had remembered later in a dream. Although half-hearted attempts were made to explain it as a struggle between the weak and the strong, it seems an irrelevant intrusion into the solemn ritual.

When the old man has gone the proper sequence centering round the mock corpse is resumed. The horns and orchestra announce a new figure, the Dorje Lopön, the leader of the Shanak, Black Hat dancers. He wears a huge black hat with a wide brim and a high crown topped by a flame ornament and a peacock's feather set in a gold jewel; a long brocade streamer flows behind it. His robes are of dark brocade with rainbow embroidery on the skirt and on the flowing sleeves; on his apron there is a Mahakala mask surrounded by *dorjes* and skulls, and he has a breastplate and necklace of bone. This role is entrusted to the most accomplished of the dancers, with a posture of dignity and authority and whose movements are graceful and fluent but also expressive of power and firm purpose. He is the hierophant for the culminating rites that follow. He dances gravely and impressively holding a *dorje* in one hand and a skull cup in the other. Soon, to a further summons by the horns, a party of monks from the Namgye Tratsang in ceremonial robes, preceded by music and carrying golden censers and ritual vessels, lead on fifteen more Black Hat dancers, who form a gyrating circle around their leader. After a while all the masked dancers who had taken part in the opening ceremonial come out, led by Shinjé, and dance in an outer circle around the Black Hats. The whole courtyard is now full of

Masked dancers with Hashang in the foreground.

movement and colour and one's senses are dazed by the swirling dance and the clamour of sound with all the players exerting the full power of their booming horns, piercing woodwinds and clashing cymbals.

There is a lull and a table is set up in the centre on which there are laid out the nine symbolic weapons for the destruction of evil—a sword, curved chopper, noose, chain, trident, a pair of skull cups, a bell, a knife, and a dagger with a *dorje* handle. The gold vessels are also set there, and the priests of the Namgye Tratsang come to perform a *serkhyem* libation ceremony with them, intoning deep-voiced prayers in which all the dancers and musicians join. They exhort the corpse to repent of the ill deeds done in the body which is about to win release through its destruction.

When the service is over the dance resumes and the Dorje Lopön approaches the table and with slow wide sweeps of his arm takes each of the weapons in turn and brandishes it over the corpse, finally pouring water and blood over it from the skull cups and plunging the dagger into its heart.

The dancers withdraw to the sides, leaving the centre clear. The orchestra strikes up a rapid rhythm and a little dancer springs down the stairs. He wears a silver brocade robe and a massive stag's head mask decorated with ribbons and paper flowers. He dances round the corpse with swift vigorous athletic movements, leaping and twirling, swaying and nodding his head, squatting on the ground and leaping lightly up in a brilliant and exciting dance. Finally he bends over the corpse with gestures of cutting it in pieces and scattering them in all directions.

Meanwhile in the south-east corner a large cauldron of oil has been heating over a brushwood fire. When the little stag's dance has finished, the Dorje Lopön dances up to it and with slow sweeping gestures pours a cup of spirit into it. There is a fierce blaze and the paper corpse is thrown onto the flames. The burning oil is then upset on to the ground and other paper images burnt in it.

The protracted rites of catharsis, ignorantly miscalled Devil Dances, are over and the participants dance slowly back to the Potala where they are able at last to shake off the intense concentration of the day.

As we too leave, a procession of monks from the Namgye Tratsang crosses the courtyard with music and tall banners. They descend the long stone stairs at the east end of the Potala to an open space near the tall pillar outside the walls of the Shö, where a pile of brushwood is waiting. There they hold a brief service; the pyre is lighted and a *torma* is cast onto it to cries of triumph and a burst of musketry from the Zimchongpa as the last traces of evil are dispelled.

30th day: The Prayers at Ramoché

ར་ཆེ་སྨོན་ལམ།

Although for the general public the Gutor on the 28th of the month is the end of the religious year, Thupten Sangay records one more, a virtually private ceremony when the monks of Sera assemble at the Ramoché temple for a day of prayer, the Raché Mönlam. It begins with a service of confession after which the morning meal is taken. Then, presided over by the Ganden Tri Rinpoché, prayer sessions continue throughout the day with intervals for tea as at the Mönlam Chenmo in the first month. The tea and also alms are provided by the Tibetan government, perhaps as some sort of compensation for the dominance over the Mönlam Chenmo by Drepung.

Epilogue

This, sadly, is an epitaph for one part of the religion, culture and the whole social order of Tibet which have been destroyed by the Chinese occupying force since 1959. The ceremonies I have described can never again be seen as they were. Tibetans in exile observe the Great Prayer and ritual dances and in Tibet the Chinese now permit the celebration of some of the festivals; but any attempt to revive the great ceremonials of Church and State would be a mere pageant. Even more tragic has been the wholesale devastation of countless monasteries, temples and even private altars in a deliberate attempt to obliterate the faith which for centuries has been the unifying spirit of the Tibetan people. Though many of the external manifestations of that faith can no longer be seen, it still lives and is strong. The Chinese now realize that to some extent and in a new policy aimed at restoring their reputation and drawing a veil over the past — and in order to cash in on tourism — have been rebuilding some of the most famous monasteries and temples vandalized or completely demolished in the Cultural Revolution; and they have been replacing with replicas the images and sacred vessels they broke up or stole.

The practice of religion which was for long proscribed is once again permitted, though under ultimate Chinese supervision and subject to restrictions on the number of monks to be admitted to monasteries and the hours for which holy places may be open. It is done in a vein of patronizing cynicism. Religion is seen as a primitive but now harmless superstition, and the temples and their furnishings are regarded as of architectural and artistic interest. Nevertheless there has survived in them something numinous, not made by hands, of which the Chinese have no comprehension, and there is poignant evidence of what their faith and the independence of their country mean to Tibetans in the thousands of men and women, monk and lay, imprisoned in brutal Chinese gaols because they have demonstrated or spoken out in defence of those natural rights.

There is widespread popular sympathy and support in many countries for the brave Tibetans in their own country and for those in exile who work to keep the Tibetan ideal alive. Unfortunately most governments have failed to live up to their responsibility to support the rights, under the Charter of the United Nations, of self-determination and the free practice of religion for the Tibetans.

Bibliography

Works in Western Languages

Beligatti, Cassiano, da Macerata, "Il giornale del P. Cassiano da Macerata", in *I missionari italiani nel Tibet e nel Nepal*, ed. Luciano Petech, 7 vols., Rome, 1952-6, iv, pp. 1-142.

Bell, Charles, *The Religion of Tibet*, London, 1931.

Betjeman, Penelope, "An Account of the Western Himalayan Bhunda Rites in the Sutlej Valley", *Saras: Bulletin of Asian Religious Art Series*, 1984.

Chapman, F. Spencer, *Lhasa, the Holy City*, London, 1938.

Das, Sarat Chandra, *Journey to Lhasa and Central Tibet*, ed. W.W. Rockhill, London, 1902.

David-Neel, Alexandra, *Voyage d'une parisienne à Lhassa*, Paris, 1929.

Harrer, Heinrich, *Lost Lhasa: Heinrich Harrer's Tibet*, New York, 1992.

Heinrich Harrer, *Seven Years in Tibet*, London, 1953.

——*Tibet: Zeitdocumente aus den Jähren 1944-1951*, Zürich, 1991.

Hayden, Henry and César Cosson, *Sport and Travel in the Highlands of Tibet*, London, 1927.

Huc, Evariste Régis and Joseph Gabet, *Travels in Tartary, Thibet and China, 1844-1846*, trans. William Hazlitt, London, 1936 edn.

Imaeda, Yoshiro, "Une note sur le rite du glud-'gon rgyal-po d'après les sources chinoises", *Journal Asiatique*, cclxvi (1978), pp. 333-9.

Karmay, Samten, "L'homme et le boeuf: le rituel de glud «rançon»", *Journal Asiatique*, cclxxix (1991), pp 327-81.

Karsten, Joachim, "A Note on *Ya Sor* and the Secular Festivals Following the *sMon lam chen mo*", *Proceedings of the Csoma de Körös Symposium*, 2 vols., Budapest, 1983, i, pp. 117-49.

Macdonald, David, *The Land of the Lama*, London, 1929.

Nebesky-Wojkowitz, René de, *Oracles and Demons of Tibet: The Cult and Iconography of the Tibetan Protective Deities*, London, 1956.

Schäfer, Ernst, *Fest der weissen Schleier*, Braunschsweig, 1949.

Shen, T.L. and Liu, S.C., *Tibet and the Tibetans*, London, 1953.

Singh, Kishen ("Pundit A.K."), Report of 1879-82, in *Exporations in Tibet and Neighbouring Regions, 1865-1892* (Records of the Survey of India, viii, 2 parts, Dehradun, 1915), pt. 2, pp. 215-323, esp. pp. 240-1.

Singh, Nain ("Chief Pundit"), Report of 1865-6, *ibid*, pt. 1, pp. 1-77, esp. pp. 20-1.

Tsybikov, G.T., *Un pèlerin bouddhiste au Tibet*, ed. and trans. Bernard Kreise, Paris, 1992.

Works in Tibetan

Chödrak, Geshe (dGe-bshes Chos-grags), *brDa-dag ming-tshig gsal-ba* [Tibetan-Tibetan-Chinese Dictionary], Beijing, 1957 edn.

Sangye Gyatso (Sangs-rgyas rGya-mtsho), *dGa'-ldan chos-'byung Beedurya ser-po* [The Religious History of Ganden (the Gelukpa School): or, The Yellow Beryl], Xining, 1989 edn.

Shankhawa, Gyurme Sonam Tobgye (Shan-kha-ba 'Gyur-med bSod-nams sTobs-rgyal), *Bod-gzhung-gi sngar-srol chos-kyi mdzad-rim* [The Sequence of Religious Ceremonies of the Tibetan State According to Ancient Custom], Library of Tibetan Works and Archives, Dharamsala, 1984.

Thupten Sangay (Thub-bstan Sangs-rgyas), *Bod-kyi dus-ston* [Festivals of Tibet], Library of Tibetan Works and Archives, Dharamsala, 1974.

Zasak Jigme Taring, (Dza-sag 'Jigs-med Phreng-ring), *lHa-sa gtsug-lag-khang-gi sa-bkra dang dkar-chag* [The Index and Plan of Lhasa Cathedral in Tibet] drawn by Zasak J. Taring from memory, Dehra Dun, 1980.

Tibetan Glossary and Index

Included here are Tibetan names, titles, terms and expressions as they appear rendered phonetically in this book. In the absence of any standardized system of representing Tibetan sounds, the one used here is inevitably subjective and not always consistent. To satisfy readers of Tibetan, each entry is followed by its proper Tibetan orthography, transliterated according to the Wylie system and contained within brackets. The root letter (*ming-gzhi*) of each segment of a name has been capitalized in the transliteration. The definitions supplied, which are far from exhaustive, are intended to be of help to the general reader.

The Heritage of Tibet

THE GREAT STUPA OF GYANTSE
A Complete Tibetan Pantheon of the Fifteenth Century
Franco Ricca & Erberto Lo Bue

CEREMONIES OF THE LHASA YEAR
Hugh Richardson

TIBETAN MEDICAL PAINTINGS
Illustrations to the Blue Beryl *Treatise of Sangye Gyamtso (1653-1705)*
Edited by Yuri Parfionovitch,
Gyurme Dorje & Fernand Meyer

INDO-TIBETAN BUDDHISM
Indian Buddhists and their Tibetan Successors
David Snellgrove

SECRET VISIONS OF
THE FIFTH DALAI LAMA
The Gold Manuscript in the Fournier Collection
Samten Karmay

EARLY TEMPLES OF CENTRAL TIBET
Roberto Vitali

TIBETAN THANGKA PAINTING
Methods & Materials
David & Janice Jackson

NOMADS OF WESTERN TIBET
The Survival of a Way of Life
Melvyn Goldstein and Cynthia Beall

JAPANESE AGENT IN TIBET
My Ten Years of Travel in Disguise
Hisao Kimura as told to Scott Berry

HIMALAYAN ENCHANTMENT
An Anthology
Frank Kingdon-Ward
Edited by John Whitehead

If you wish to receive our catalogue please write to:

Serindia Publications
10 Parkfields
London SW15 6NH, UK

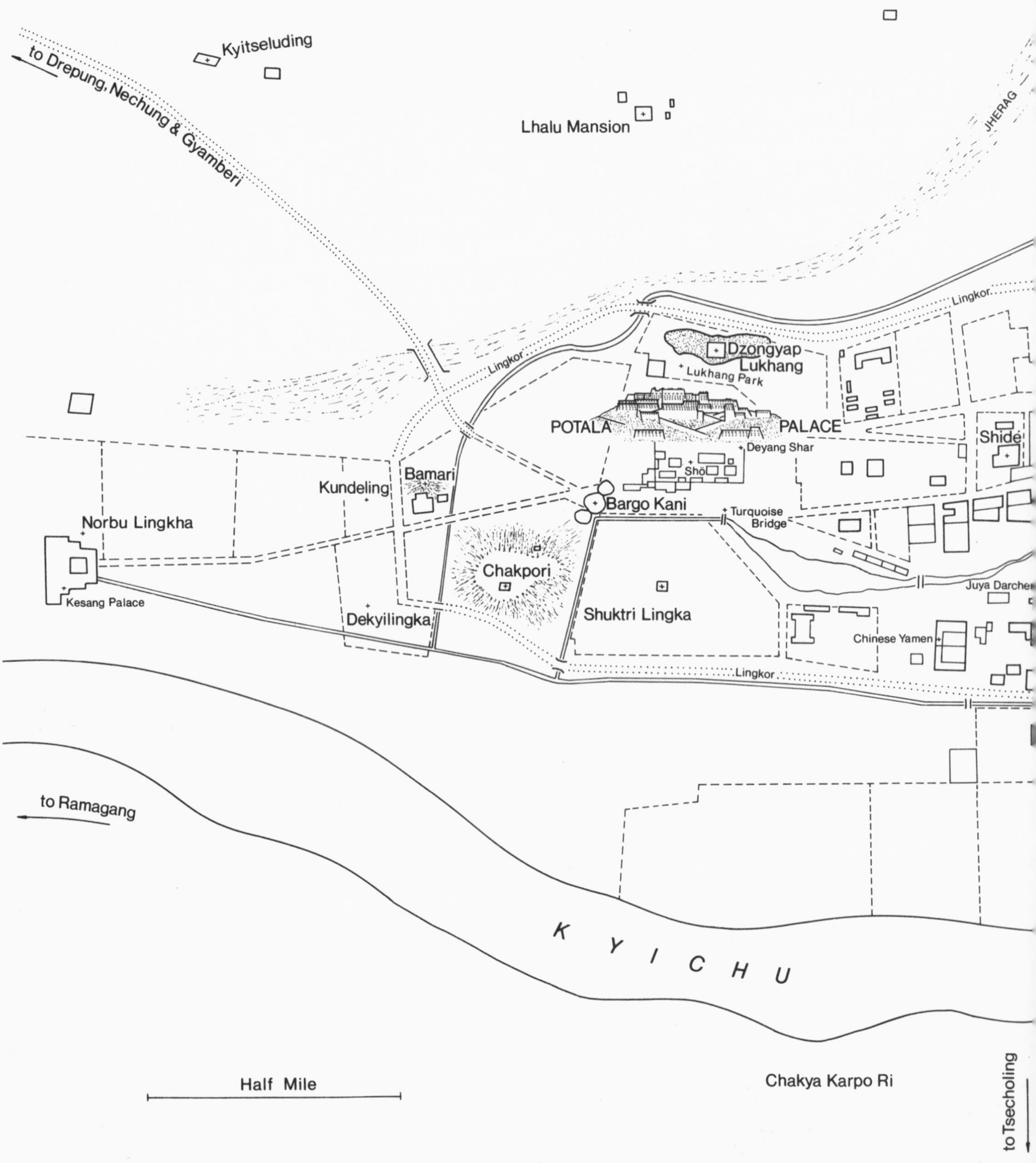

Kyitseluding
to Drepung, Nechung & Gyamberi
Lhalu Mansion
JHERAG
Lingkor
Dzongyap
Lukhang
Lukhang Park
POTALA
PALACE
Deyang Shar
Shö
Shidé
Bamari
Kundeling
Bargo Kani
Turquoise
Bridge
Norbu Lingkha
Chakpori
Juya Darcher
Kesang Palace
Dekyilingka
Shuktri Lingka
Chinese Yamen
Lingkor
to Ramagang
K Y I C H U
Half Mile
Chakya Karpo Ri
to Tsecholing

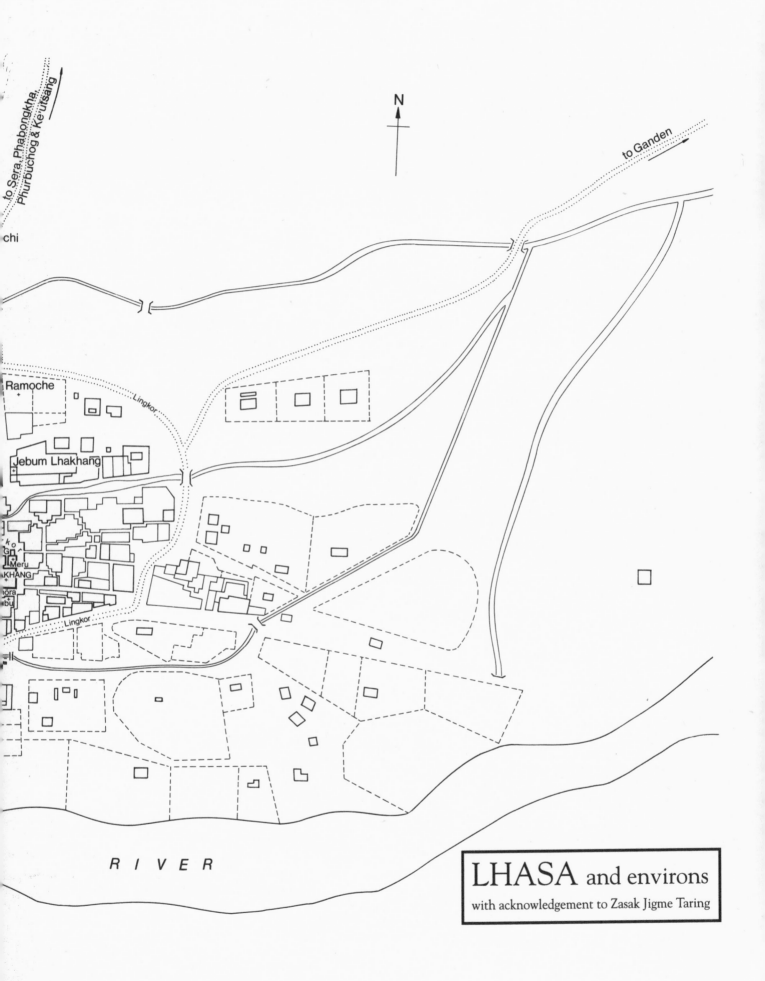

to Sera, Phabongkha, Phurbuchog & Ke'utsang
N
to Ganden
chi
Ramoche
Lingkor
Jebum Lhakhang
Meru
KHANG
Lingkor
RIVER
LHASA and environs
with acknowledgement to Zasak Jigme Taring